KU-390-769

HAMLYN ALL COLOUR SALADS

HAMLYN ALL COLOUR SALADS

TED SMART

Front cover shows, left to right:
Salad Niçoise (recipe 65), Curried Chicken
Mayonnaise (recipe 133), Avocado Salad
with Oregano (recipe 1).

Back cover shows, clockwise from top left:
Hummous (recipe 157), Pasta, Pea and Artichoke
Salad (recipe 89), Yogurt Sauce with Herbs
(recipe 213), Honeydew Melon Salad (recipe 177),
Sweet and Sour Salad (recipe 41)

Illustrations by Sandra Pond and Will Giles

First published 1992
Hamlyn is an imprint of Octopus Illustrated Publishing
Michelin House, 81 Fulham Road, London SW3 6RB
part of Reed International Books Limited

A catalogue record of this book is available
from the British Library

ISBN 1 85613 113 0

Produced by Mandarin Offset
Printed in Hong Kong

Contents

USEFUL FACTS AND FIGURES

NOTES ON METRICATION

In this book quantities are given in metric and Imperial measures. Exact conversion from Imperial to metric measures does not usually give very convenient working quantities and so the metric measures have been rounded off into units of 25 grams. The table below shows the recommended equivalents.

Ounces	*Approx g to nearest whole figure*	*Recommended conversion to nearest unit of 25*	*Ounces*	*Approx g to nearest whole figure*	*Recommended conversion to nearest unit of 25*
1	28	25	9	255	250
2	57	50	10	283	275
3	85	75	11	312	300
4	113	100	12	340	350
5	142	150	13	368	375
6	170	175	14	396	400
7	198	200	15	425	425
8	227	225	16(1lb)	454	450

Note

When converting quantities over 16 oz first add the appropriate figures in the centre column, then adjust to the nearest unit of 25. As a general guide, 1kg (1000 g) equals 2.2 lb or about 2 lb 3 oz. This method of conversion gives good results in nearly all cases, although in certain pastry and cake recipes a more accurate conversion is necessary to produce a balanced recipe.

Liquid measures

The millilitre has been used in this book and the following table gives a few examples.

Imperial	*Approx ml to nearest whole figure*	*Recommended ml*	*Imperial*	*Approx ml to nearest whole figure*	*Recommended ml*
1/4	142	150 ml	1 pint	567	600 ml
1/2	283	300 ml	1 1/2 pints	851	900 ml
3/4	425	450 ml	1 3/4 pints	992	1000 ml (1 litre)

Spoon measures

All spoon measures given in this book are level unless otherwise stated.

Can sizes

At present, cans are marked with the exact (usually to the nearest whole number) metric equivalent of the Imperial weight of the contents, so we have followed this practice when giving can sizes.

Oven temperatures

The table below gives recommended equivalents.

	°C	°F	Gas Mark		°C	°F	Gas Mark
Very cool	110	225	1/4	Moderately hot	190	375	5
	120	250	1/2		200	400	6
Cool	140	275	1	Hot	220	425	7
	150	300	2		230	450	8
Moderate	160	325	3	Very hot	240	475	9
	180	350	4				

NOTES FOR AMERICAN AND AUSTRALIAN USERS

In America the 8-fl oz measuring cup is used. In Australia metric measures are now used in conjunction with the standard 250-ml measuring cup. The Imperial pint, used in Britain and Australia, is 20 fl oz, while the American pint is 16 fl oz. It is important to remember that the Australian tablespoon differs from both the British and American tablespoons; the table below gives a comparison. The British standard tablespoon, which has been used throughout this book, holds 17.7 ml, the American 14.2 ml, and the Australian 20 ml. A teaspoon holds approximately 5 ml in all three countries.

British	*American*	*Australian*
1 teaspoon	1 teaspoon	1 teaspoon
1 tablespoon	1 tablespoon	1 tablespoon
2 tablespoons	3 tablespoons	2 tablespoons
3 1/2 tablespoons	4 tablespoons	3 tablespoons
4 tablespoons	5 tablespoons	3 1/2 tablespoons

AN IMPERIAL/AMERICAN GUIDE TO SOLID AND LIQUID MEASURES

Imperial	*American*	*Imperial*	*American*
Solid measures		Liquid measures	
1 lb butter or margarine	2 cups	1/4 pint liquid	2/3 cup liquid
		1/2 pint	1 1/4 cups
1lb flour	4 cups	3/4 pint	2 cups
1 lb granulated or caster sugar	2 cups	1 pint	2 1/2 cups
		1 1/2 pints	3 3/4 cups
1lb icing sugar	3 cups	2 pints	5 cups (2 1/2 pints)
8 oz rice	1 cup		

NOTE: WHEN MAKING ANY OF THE RECIPES IN THIS BOOK, ONLY FOLLOW ONE SET OF MEASURES AS THEY ARE NOT INTERCHANGEABLE.

INTRODUCTION

A good salad is a dish in its own right, not just an accompaniment for other foods. For health-conscious cooks, salads are also all-year-round dishes, providing satisfying meals in winter as often as in summer.

HAMLYN ALL COLOUR SALADS contains 240 recipes which make full use of the enormous range of potential salad ingredients available in our shops and supermarkets. Vegetables and fruits from all parts of the world, seafood from the seven seas, meats and poultry of all kinds, fresh herbs, exotic spices and flavourings are combined in wonderfully imaginative ways, their flavours enhanced by carefully chosen dressings or mayonnaises.

The salads have been planned with all kinds of meals in mind. The opening chapter, for instance, is a collection of recipes for salads with which to begin a meal: the sort of dish, not too large or heavy on ingredients, which whets the appetite.

There is a chapter of salads where the main ingredients, combined with a surprising variety of other foods, are eggs and cheeses of all kinds, which provide good nutrition and an interesting contrast in textures. Turn from these to the chapter called 'World Choice' to find a deliciously different array of salads from all round the world; exotic they may be, but their ingredients are all available here.

'Mainly Vegetables' makes good use of the wonderful variety of texture, colour and taste offered by vegetables, while 'Main Course Salads', as its name indicates, is a collection of salads able to hold their own as the centrepiece of a meal. To follow, some salads based on those invaluable staple foods, pulses and grains, as well as pasta, and 'Mainly Fruit' shows the great versatility of fruit as an ingredient for salads to be served at all stages of a meal. The choice of dressing or mayonnaise can change the character of the simplest salad, and the final chapter of this book provides a wide-ranging choice of ways to dress a salad.

The recipes in this book, and the full-colour photograph which accompanies each one, are intended as inspiration for cooks, providing the jumping-off point from which to create their own, unique salads. With the exception of one or two 'classic' salads, there are very few salads here which cannot be experimented with, or their ingredients changed to suit what is available in shops or storecupboard.

The Cook's Tips which accompany the recipes add up to much additional useful information, making this book so much more than just a collection of recipes, while calorie counts for all recipes help greatly in the business of planning well-balanced meals.

FIRST COURSE SALADS

This imaginative selection of salads, based on a wide range of ingredients, offers stylish starters for all meals, from simple suppers to grand dinners.

1 AVOCADO SALAD WITH OREGANO

Preparation time:
20 minutes

Serves 4

Calories:
555 per portion

YOU WILL NEED:
2 avocados
4 large lettuce leaves
4 tomatoes
175-200 g/6-7 oz mozzarella cheese
salt and pepper
6 tablespoons olive oil
2 tablespoons white wine vinegar
1 teaspoon dried oregano

Cut the avocados in half, peel them and remove the stones. Lay a lettuce leaf on each plate and put half an avocado on it cut side down. Run a knife lengthways down the centre of the avocado, then cut it across in slices.

Skin the tomatoes and cut them in half. Slice each half, and lay the slices on either side of the avocados.

Cut the mozzarella cheese in thin slices and arrange between the tomato slices. Sprinkle with salt and pepper.

Mix the oil and vinegar together and dribble over the salad, then scatter a pinch of dried oregano over each plate. Serve immediately.

COOK'S TIP

Avocados tend to bruise easily, turning part of the flesh black, so handle with care. The variety with the crinkly skin is rather less prone to being bruised.

2 AVOCADO SALAD WITH CORIANDER

Preparation time:
20 minutes

Serves 4

Calories:
320 per portion

YOU WILL NEED:
2 large ripe avocados, peeled, stoned and diced
350 g/12 oz tomatoes, skinned, seeded, drained and chopped
2 bunches spring onions, sliced
dash of Tabasco sauce (optional)
1 tablespoon lemon juice
1 tablespoon fresh lime juice
2 tablespoons sunflower oil
2 tablespoons chopped fresh coriander
salt and pepper
lime slices, to garnish

Combine the avocados, tomatoes and spring onions in a bowl. Add the Tabasco sauce, if using, the lemon and lime juices, oil and coriander. Stir lightly but thoroughly to mix well and season to taste with salt and pepper. Garnish with lime slices and serve.

COOK'S TIP

You may find it better to halve the avocados and remove the stone before peeling. If the avocados are chilled lightly, the flesh will be easier to dice neatly.

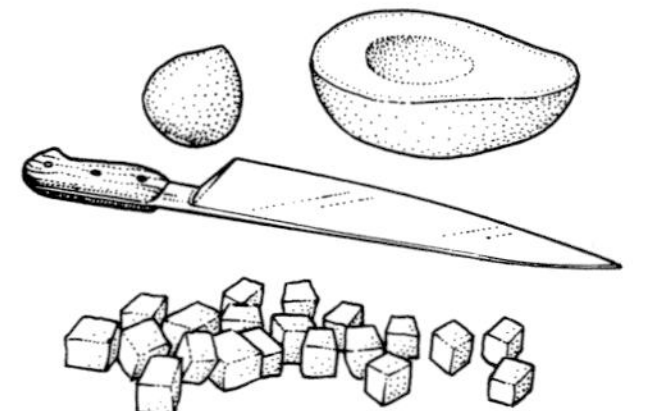

3 SPINACH, AVOCADO AND WALNUT SALAD

Preparation time:
20 minutes

Serves 4

Calories:
264 per portion

YOU WILL NEED:
450 g/1 lb young spinach, trimmed
100 g/4 oz lean ham
1 small avocado, peeled, stoned and sliced
50 g/2 oz walnuts
1 small orange, peeled and sliced
dressing, to serve (see Cook's Tip)

Roughly tear the spinach leaves and place in a salad bowl.

Cut the ham into strips and add to the spinach with the avocado and walnuts. Arrange the orange slices on top. Serve the chosen dressing separately.

COOK'S TIP

A delicious dressing to serve with this salad is Orange vinaigrette (see recipe 227). It complements the flavours better than French dressing would.

4 AVOCADO WITH PEARS AND BLACK OLIVES

Preparation time:
15 minutes

Serves 4

Calories:
337 per portion

YOU WILL NEED:
2 avocados
2 tablespoons lemon juice
6 large black olives
1½ tablespoons Mayonnaise (see recipe 219)
1 x 200 g/7 oz can pear quarters, drained and diced
salt and pepper

Halve the avocados, discard the stones and rub with a little of the lemon juice to prevent discoloration.

Halve the olives and discard the stones. Set aside 4 halves for garnish; chop the remainder.

Mix the mayonnaise and remaining lemon juice together in a bowl. Add the diced pears, chopped olives, and salt and pepper to taste.

Pile the mixture into the avocado halves. Garnish each portion with an olive half.

COOK'S TIP

Buy pears that have been canned in unsweetened fruit juice rather than syrup as this makes the fruit still taste sweetened even after it has been carefully drained.

5 AVOCADO WITH GREEN HERB DRESSING

Preparation time:
10 minutes

Serves 4

Calories:
574 per portion

YOU WILL NEED:
2 avocados
100 g/4 oz frozen peeled prawns, thawed
4 tablespoons Green herb dressing (see recipe 236)

Halve the pears and remove the stones. Scoop out the flesh and cut into neat pieces. Place in a bowl with the prawns and dressing.

Mix together carefully and spoon into 4 individual serving dishes. Serve with wholemeal bread and butter.

COOK'S TIP

Cover the avocado pieces with the dressing as soon as possible after cutting them, to prevent discoloration. If the salad has to sit a while before serving, cover the dishes tightly with cling film.

6 MUSHROOM, COURGETTE AND TOMATO SALAD

Preparation time:
15 minutes

Serves 4

Calories:
132 per portion

YOU WILL NEED:
6 large mushrooms, sliced
4 courgettes, peeled and thinly sliced
4 tomatoes, skinned and quartered
3 tablespoons French dressing (see recipe 233)
1 bunch watercress
1 teaspoon chopped fresh basil

Mix the mushrooms, courgettes and tomatoes together. Spoon over the dressing and turn the vegetables over in it. Arrange the watercress in a serving dish and put the courgette mixture in the centre. Sprinkle the chopped basil over it.

COOK'S TIP

For a lower calorie salad use a Lemon vinaigrette (recipe 227) instead of the basic French dressing.

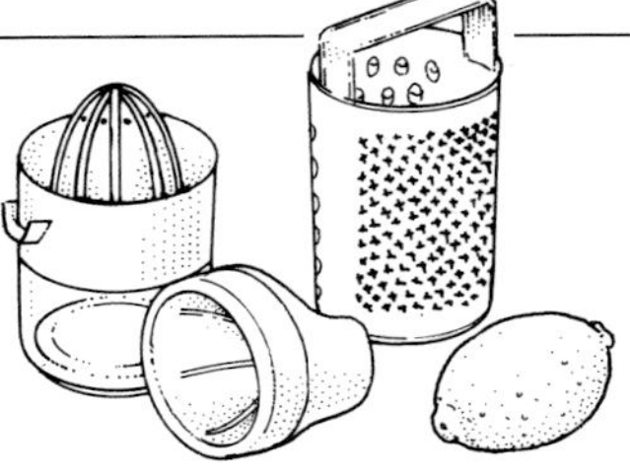

7 MUSHROOM AND BEANSHOOT SALAD

Preparation time:
10 minutes, plus marinating

Serves 4

Calories:
123 per portion

YOU WILL NEED:
350 g/12 oz button mushrooms
6 tablespoons French dressing (see recipe 233)
250 g/8 oz beanshoots
1 red pepper, cored, seeded and finely sliced

Cut the mushrooms into quarters and place in a salad bowl. Add the dressing and toss well. Leave to marinate for 1 hour, stirring occasionally.

Add the beanshoots and sliced red pepper. Toss thoroughly before serving.

COOK'S TIP

Beanshoots are a valuable source of vitamins. It takes only a few days for sprouting seeds to grow in jars (see recipe 120).

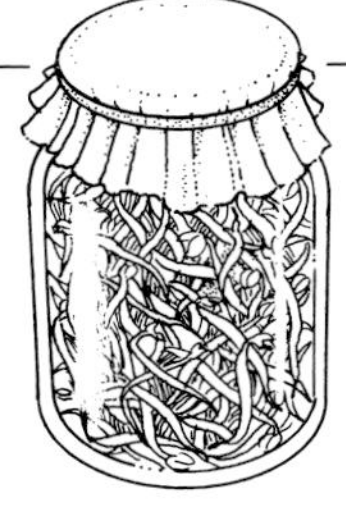

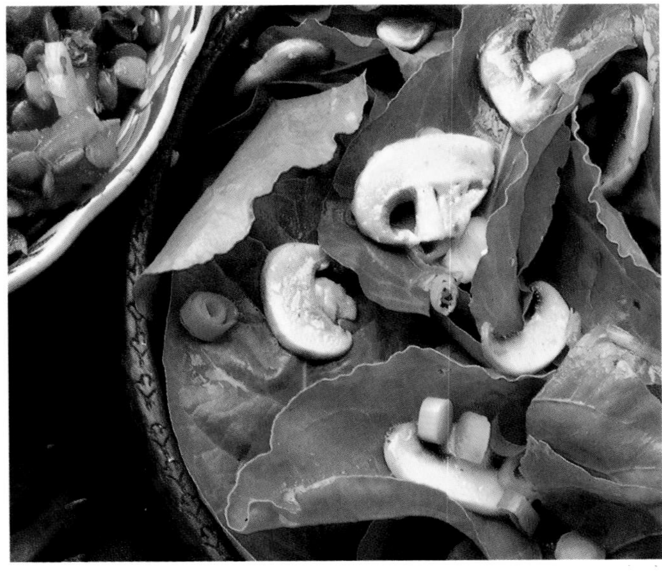

8 SPINACH AND MUSHROOM SALAD

Preparation time:
10 minutes, plus marinating

Serves 4

Calories:
116 per portion

YOU WILL NEED:
250 g/8 oz button mushrooms, sliced
4 tablespoons French dressing (see recipe 233)
250 g/8 oz young spinach leaves
4 spring onions, chopped

Place the mushrooms in a bowl, add 3 tablespoons of the dressing and toss well. Leave to marinate for 1 hour, stirring occasionally.

Wash and thoroughly dry the spinach. Discard the thick centre stalks and tear the leaves into a salad bowl. Add the marinated mushrooms, spring onions and remaining dressing. Toss well to serve.

COOK'S TIP

It is not necessary to peel the mushrooms unless the skin is blemished. Just place in a sieve and rinse under a trickling tap.

9 FENNEL SALAD

Preparation time:
15 minutes

Serves 4

Calories:
173 per portion

YOU WILL NEED:
1 small lettuce heart, shredded
2 medium fennel bulbs, thinly sliced
2 oranges, peeled and thinly sliced into rings
1 bunch watercress
50 g/2 oz currants
50 g/2 oz walnut halves
FOR THE DRESSING
3 tablespoons sunflower oil
1 tablespoon orange juice
1 tablespoon orange rind
1 teaspoon red wine vinegar
salt and pepper
1 tablespoon sunflower seeds, crushed
chopped walnuts, to garnish

Put the dressing ingredients in a screw-top jar and shake well together to mix.

Toss the lettuce and fennel together.

Make a ring of the orange slices around the outside of a dish. Arrange the watercress sprigs in a ring inside them.

Just before serving the salad, toss the lettuce and fennel in the dressing and pile the salad in the centre of the orange and watercress rings. Make a ring of currants around the green salad. Scatter the walnuts on top.

COOK'S TIP

The ingredients for this salad, including the dressing, may be prepared 2-3 hours before the meal and kept, covered, in the refrigerator until required.

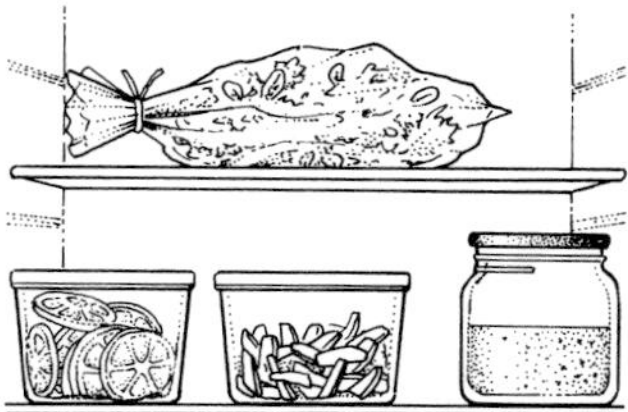

10 FENNEL AND CORIANDER OLIVE SALAD

Preparation time:
10 minutes

Serves 4

Calories:
175 per portion

YOU WILL NEED:
2 bulbs fresh fennel, about 450 g/1 lb total weight
100 g/4 oz coriander-stuffed or 'cracked' olives
4 tablespoons olive oil
1 tablespoon white wine vinegar
1 tablespoon orange juice
salt and pepper

Cut off the feathery leaves from the fennel bulbs, chop these and reserve. Trim the root end of each bulb and any small tough stalks at the top. Finely slice the rest of the bulb and place in a salad dish.

If using coriander-stuffed or 'cracked' olives which have not been stoned, stone them taking care not to brush off all the coriander seeds. Scatter the olives over the fennel strips.

Mix together the oil, vinegar and orange juice, either shaking in a screw-top jar or whisking until the mixture is well blended. Pour over the salad and season with salt and pepper. Garnish with the reserved fennel leaves.

COOK'S TIP

Coriander-stuffed olives are sold in Greek food shops. Alternatively, stone large green olives, then make a slit from one end half-way down and pack in layers in a jar. Sprinkle each layer with about 4 teaspoons crushed coriander seeds to 100 g/4 oz olives. Cover with olive oil. Cover the jar tightly and leave for at least a week.

11 FENNEL AND TOMATOES WITH DILL

Preparation time:
20 minutes, plus standing

Cooking time:
15-20 minutes

Serves 4

Calories:
80 per portion

YOU WILL NEED:
4 small bulbs fresh fennel
sunflower oil or groundnut oil for frying
salt and pepper
450 g/1 lb tomatoes
3 tablespoons chopped fresh dill

Cut the fennel into very thin vertical slices. Heat enough oil to cover the bottom of a heavy pan and stew the fennel gently, stirring often, until almost soft. Add plenty of salt and pepper. Skin and slice the tomatoes. Add them to the fennel and continue to cook gently for 5 minutes, stirring occasionally very carefully with a spatula, to avoid breaking up the tomatoes. When ready, stir in the chopped dill and turn into a dish to cool. Serve cold, but do not chill.

COOK'S TIP

The flavour of this salad seems to improve on standing, so it is better made a day in advance and kept in a cool place, not in the refrigerator.

12 TOMATO, CUCUMBER AND FENNEL SALAD

Preparation time:
20 minutes

Serves 6

Calories:
54 per portion

YOU WILL NEED:
350 g/12 oz tomatoes
½ cucumber
½ small fennel bulb, about 100 g/4 oz
salt and pepper
2 tablespoons olive oil
½ tablespoon white wine vinegar
½ tablespoon lemon juice

Skin the tomatoes and slice them thinly. Lay them on a flat dish. Peel the cucumber, slice it thinly and lay over the tomatoes. Cut the fennel in thin horizontal slices and scatter over the cucumber, reserving the feathery leaves. Sprinkle with salt and pepper.

Mix the oil, vinegar and lemon juice in a bowl and pour over the salad. Chop the fennel leaves and scatter them on top.

COOK'S TIP

Do not discard the root end and any small tough stalks at the top of the fennel bulb. Reserve for flavouring stocks, soups or fish dishes.

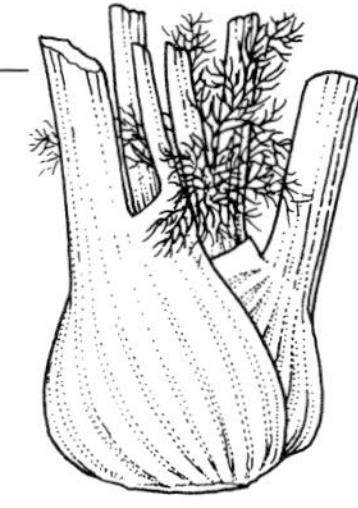

13 TOMATO AND MOZZARELLA SALAD WITH BASIL

Preparation time:
15 minutes, plus standing

Serves 4

Calories:
281 per portion

YOU WILL NEED:
450g/1 lb tomatoes
225 g/8 oz Mozzarella cheese
salt and pepper
3 tablespoons olive oil
1 tablespoon white wine vinegar
1½ tablespoons chopped fresh basil

Skin the tomatoes and slice them thinly and evenly. Lay them on one half of a flat serving dish. Cut the cheese into thin slices and lay them on the other half of the same dish.

Season the tomatoes with salt and pepper, the Mozzarella with pepper only. Pour over the oil and vinegar and scatter the chopped basil on top. Allow the salad to stand for a little before serving.

■ COOK'S TIP

The Italian bread called ciabatta makes an ideal accompaniment for this salad. If possible, buy the ready-to-bake version and serve it warm.

14 TOMATOES WITH HORSERADISH MAYONNAISE

Preparation time:
10 minutes

Serves 4

Calories:
144 per portion, plus cream

YOU WILL NEED:
4 large tomatoes, sliced
3 tablespoons Mayonnaise (see recipe 219)
1 tablespoon creamed horseradish
1-2 tablespoons single cream (optional)
chopped parsley, to garnish

Arrange the tomatoes neatly in a serving dish. Mix the mayonnaise with the horseradish, adding a little cream if necessary to give the consistency of tnick cream.

Spoon the dressing over the tomatoes and sprinkle with chopped parsley before serving.

■ COOK'S TIP

To chop parsley quickly, hold the handle of the knife in one hand and the tip in the other. This is how chefs do it!

15 STUFFED ICEBERG LETTUCE

Preparation time:
15-20 minutes, plus chilling

Serves 4-6

Calories:
259-173 per portion

YOU WILL NEED:
1 iceberg lettuce, trimmed
175 g/6 oz full fat soft cheese, curd cheese or quark
2 tablespoons milk
25 g/1 oz sultanas
25 g/1 oz walnuts, chopped
1 red pepper, cored, seeded and diced
salt and pepper

Cut off the top of the lettuce and reserve, for the lid. Using a small sharp knife, scoop out the inside, leaving a 2.5 cm/1 inch thick case.

Chop the scooped-out lettuce very finely and place in a large bowl.

In a bowl, beat the soft cheese with the milk until smooth. Stir in the sultanas, walnuts and red pepper. Season to taste. Add the chopped lettuce and stir well to mix.

Pile the mixture into the lettuce case and replace the lid. Chill for 30 minutes before serving.

COOK'S TIP

Turn this spectacular-looking first course salad into a main meal by serving it with cold meat or chicken, or with crusty French bread.

16 ICEBERG AND COURGETTE SALAD WITH STILTON DRESSING

Preparation time:
10-15 minutes

Serves 4

Calories:
124 per portion

YOU WILL NEED:
1 small or ½ large iceberg lettuce
2 courgettes, each about 10 cm/4 inches long
½ small onion, finely chopped
4 tablespoons finely chopped parsley
FOR THE DRESSING
3 tablespoons crumbled blue Stilton cheese
3 tablespoons olive oil
2 tablespoons white wine vinegar
3 tablespoons natural yogurt
salt and pepper

Wash the lettuce, drain thoroughly, then shred it finely and put into a large salad bowl.

Wash, top and tail the courgettes but do not peel them. Slice them finely and add to the lettuce, together with the onion and chopped parsley.

Pound the crumbled Stilton with 1 tablespoon of the oil to a smooth paste, then gradually add the remaining oil, stirring vigorously all the time. Whisk in the vinegar and yogurt and stir until well blended.

Pour the dressing over the salad, tossing thoroughly to coat everything, then sprinkle with salt and pepper. Chill up to 1 hour before serving.

COOK'S TIP

An ideal recipe for using up leftover Stilton, this is also a cool and refreshing salad, good to serve at a hot summer's barbecue in the garden.

17 BEETROOT AND HORSERADISH SALAD

Preparation time:
10 minutes

Serves 4

Calories:
71 per portion

YOU WILL NEED:
2 heads chicory
4 medium cooked beetroots, peeled and diced
2 tablespoons low-calorie mayonnaise
2 teaspoons grated horseradish
1 teaspoon mustard powder

Line a serving dish with the chicory leaves. Spoon the beetroot in the centre.

Mix the mayonnaise, horseradish and mustard together and spoon on top of the beetroot.

COOK'S TIP

When buying cooked beetroot for this recipe, choose ones that have not been cooked in vinegar. Use a commercially prepared low-calorie mayonnaise.

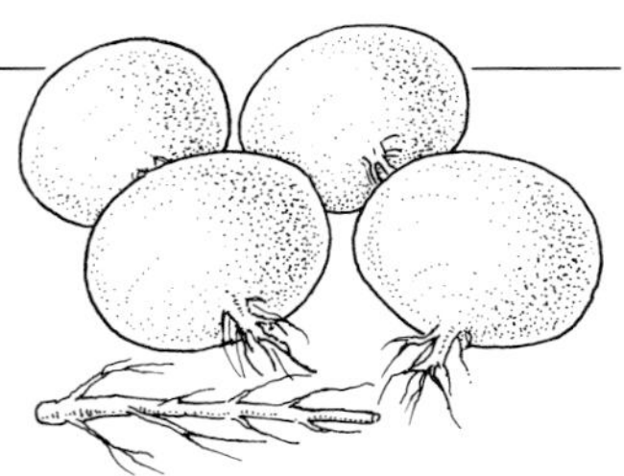

18 FRESH BEETROOT SALAD

Preparation time:
15 minutes, plus chilling

Serves 4

Calories:
50 per portion

YOU WILL NEED:
2 teaspoons olive oil
2 teaspoons lemon juice
1 teaspoon made mustard (see Cook's Tip)
3-4 small uncooked beetroots, peeled and coarsely grated
1 cucumber, peeled and sliced
1 tablespoon chopped fresh mixed herbs

Mix the olive oil, lemon juice and mustard together. Stir into the beetroot.

Arrange the cucumber slices round the edge of a shallow dish.

Put the beetroot mixture in the centre. Scatter over the herbs. Chill before serving.

COOK'S TIP

Use either a made English mustard, for a sharp flavour, or a smooth Dijon mustard, for a less hot, more sweet flavour.

19 MIXED VEGETABLE SALAD

Preparation time:
15 minutes

Cooking time:
about 20 minutes

Serves 4

Calories:
259 per portion

YOU WILL NEED:
4 carrots, peeled
225 g/8 oz potatoes, peeled
salt
225 g/8 oz peas
225 g/8 oz shelled broad beans
Lemon vinaigrette (see recipe 227), to serve

Dice the carrots and potatoes. Cook in boiling salted water for about 10 minutes until just cooked but still firm.

Meanwhile, cook the peas in boiling salted water for 6-12 minutes, depending on whether frozen or fresh, until tender.

Cook the broad beans in boiling salted water for about 15 minutes until tender.

Mix all the vegetables together in a salad bowl. Serve the Lemon vinaigrette separately, in a jug.

COOK'S TIP

This salad may be served warm, or allowed to cool before serving. Serve it with warm wholemeal bread for a satisfying starter.

20 CELERY REMOULADE

Preparation time:
20 minutes

Serves 6

Calories:
`34 per portion

YOU WILL NEED:
2 heads celery, trimmed and cut into matchstick strips, with leaves removed
FOR THE SAUCE
2 hard-boiled egg yolks
2 egg yolks
1 tablespoon Dijon mustard
salt and pepper
2 tablespoons white wine vinegar
2 tablespoons tarragon vinegar
300 ml/½ pint sunflower oil
150 ml/¼ pint soured cream

To make the remoulade sauce, place the hard-boiled egg yolks in a bowl and mash well with a fork. Using a wooden spoon, beat in the raw egg yolks and continue to beat to make a smooth paste. Beat in the mustard and season with salt and pepper. Add the vinegar very gradually, beating well between each addition until thoroughly blended. Add half the oil drop by drop, as if making mayonnaise. Add the remaining oil in a steady trickle, stirring constantly. Fold in the soured cream.

Taste the sauce and adjust the seasoning if necessary. Add the celery strips and stir well to combine. Turn the celery mixture into a serving dish and garnish with the celery leaves.

COOK'S TIP

Try adding some fresh herbs to the remoulade sauce and serving it with mussels as a starter for a dinner party. Melba toast makes a good accompaniment.

21 BACON AND RADISH SALAD

Preparation time:
20 minutes

Cooking time:
8-10 minutes

Serves 4

Calories:
146 per portion

YOU WILL NEED:
4 rashers rindless lean bacon
4 celery sticks
24 large radishes
3 tablespoons French dressing (see recipe 233)
2 teaspoons finely chopped fresh sage
watercress sprig, to garnish

Cook the bacon under a preheated grill until crisp, then drain on absorbent kitchen paper and chop into small pieces. Cut the celery and radishes into slices about 5 mm/¼ inch thick. Combine with the bacon.

Mix the dressing with the chopped sage, add to the bacon mixture. Toss lightly to coat and serve at once garnished with a sprig of watercress.

COOK'S TIP

The best way to clean celery is with a toothbrush, reserved for this purpose. Brush under cold running water to remove any particles of earth.

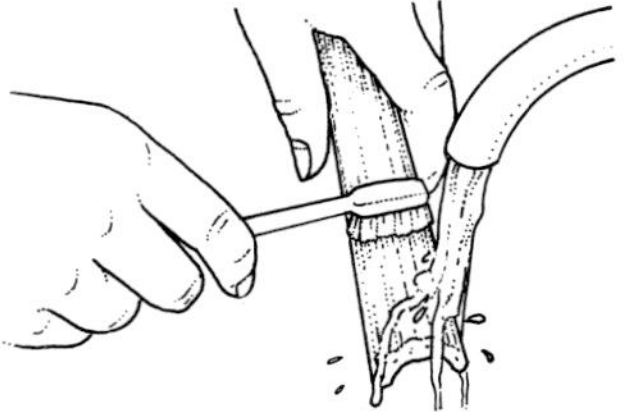

22 BACON, WALNUT AND ENDIVE SALAD

Preparation time:
15 minutes, plus standing

Cooking time:
10 minutes

Serves 4

Calories:
178 per portion

YOU WILL NEED:
4 rashers rindless streaky bacon, about 100 g/4 oz
1 curly endive, coarsely shredded
50 g/2 oz walnut halves, coarsely chopped
3 tablespoons walnut oil
2 tablespoons lemon juice
salt and pepper

Cook the bacon under a preheated grill for about 5 minutes on each side until crispy. Cool for 1-2 minutes, then crumble.

Put the shredded endive into a salad bowl, add the bacon and the walnuts. Sprinkle over the walnut oil and lemon juice and toss gently. Season lightly with salt and generously with pepper.

Keep the salad covered, but not chilled, for up to 1 hour before serving to bring out the flavours.

COOK'S TIP

Walnut oil is one of the more expensive oils but it is ideal for this salad. It is available at most major supermarkets and delicatessens.

23 ARTICHOKE HEART AND BACON SALAD

Preparation time:
10 minutes

Cooking time:
10 minutes

Serves 4

Calories:
156 per portion

YOU WILL NEED:
2 x 400 g/14 oz cans artichoke hearts, drained
4 tablespoons French dressing (see recipe 233)
50 g/2 oz rindless lean thick bacon rashers

Toss the artichoke hearts in the French dressing and arrange in a serving dish.

Cut the bacon into strips. Place a frying pan over a moderate heat, add the bacon and fry in its own fat until crisp. Cool for 1-2 minutes.

Crumble the bacon and sprinkle over the salad. Serve immediately.

COOK'S TIP

Canned artichoke hearts are an invaluable part of a good store-cupboard. They can be used to make a great variety of starters quickly.

24 PARMA HAM WITH PARMESAN AND MUSHROOMS

Preparation time:
15 minutes

Serves 6

Calories:
372 per portion

YOU WILL NEED:
350 g/12 oz Parma ham, cut very thinly
100 g/4 oz fresh Parmesan cheese, in one piece
50 g/2 oz tiny button mushrooms, very finely sliced
175 ml/ 6 fl oz olive oil
pepper

Arrange the ham on 6 individual serving plates, spreading the slices over each plate and overlapping them very slightly.

Using a sharp knife, cut very fine slivers off the cheese. Sprinkle the cheese slivers all over the ham.

Scatter the finely sliced mushrooms over the ham and then dribble about 2 tablespoons olive oil over each portion.

Sprinkle generously with pepper and serve with Melba toast and chilled butter, if liked.

COOK'S TIP

Parmesan cheese will not cut easily unless it is very fresh, so it is best to buy it from an Italian food shop. Be careful not to grate the cheese when cutting the slivers. If you do, some of the pungency of the cheese will be lost.

25 STUFFED TOMATOES

Preparation time:
20 minutes, plus chilling

Serves 4

Calories:
288 per portion

YOU WILL NEED:
1 x 450 g/1 lb can pink salmon, drained
1 celery stick, chopped
2 tablespoons finely chopped onion
2 tablespoons finely chopped green pepper
3 tablespoons French dressing (see recipe 233)
salt and pepper
4 large tomatoes
lettuce
4 lemon slices, to garnish

Flake the salmon into a bowl, discarding the skin and bone. Add the celery, onion, green pepper, dressing and seasoning to taste. Mix well and chill.

With stem end down, divide each tomato into 6 wedges, cutting down to, but not through, the base. Ease the wedges apart slightly and sprinkle lightly with salt. Spoon equal amounts of the salmon mixture into the centre of each tomato.

Serve on individual plates, garnished with a twist of lemon.

COOK'S TIP

Choose tomatoes that are ripe but still firm so that they hold their shape when divided into wedges. If liked, remove the seeds before filling with the salmon.

26 CRUNCHY SALMON SALAD

Preparation time:
15 minutes

Serves 6

Calories:
342 per portion

YOU WILL NEED:
3 tablespoons Mayonnaise (see recipe 219)
4 tablespoons lemon juice
2 x 200 g/7 oz cans red salmon
2 dessert apples, peeled, cored and diced
175 g/6 oz salted peanuts, chopped
salt and pepper
lettuce leaves

Mix the mayonnaise and lemon juice together in a bowl. Drain the salmon thoroughly, flake and add to the mayonnaise. Stir in the apples, peanuts and salt and pepper to taste.

Line a serving dish with lettuce leaves and pile the salmon mixture into the centre.

COOK'S TIP

Remember to season very lightly with salt. You may prefer to use an unsalted variety of peanut in this salad.

27 SEAFOOD COCKTAIL SALAD

Preparation time:
20 minutes

Cooking time:
4-5 minutes

Serves 4

Calories:
62 per portion

YOU WILL NEED:
4 scallops, prepared
100 g/4 oz white fish
100 g/4 oz peeled, cooked prawns
shredded lettuce leaves
8 tomatoes, skinned and quartered
FOR THE SAUCE
120 ml/4 fl oz low-calorie Mayonnaise
2 teaspoons tomato purée
1 teaspoon chopped fresh basil
salt and pepper

Place the scallops and white fish in a saucepan. Poach in the minimum of water for about 4-5 minutes until tender. Drain and cool.

Flake the fish using a fork. Cut the scallops into small pieces. Add the prawns to the fish mixture.

Mix the mayonnaise, tomato purée, basil, salt and pepper together, then stir into the fish.

Arrange the shredded lettuce on a serving dish and surround with the tomato quarters. Spoon the fish mixture into the centre of the dish.

COOK'S TIP

If you need to prepare the scallops yourself, just cut off the little strip of skin and muscle from the outside of the white part. Rinse the white part and the red coral to remove any sand and drain well.

28 SEVICHE OF SCALLOPS WITH HERBS

Preparation time:
25 minutes, plus chilling overnight

Serves 4

Calories:
73 per portion

YOU WILL NEED:
10 large scallops
4 scallop shells
150 ml/¼ pint lemon juice
1½ tablespoons very finely chopped shallot
½ tablespoon very finely chopped fresh tarragon
½ tablespoon very finely chopped fresh dill
½ tablespoon very finely chopped chives
½ tablespoon very finely chopped parsley
1½ tablespoons sunflower oil

Detach the scallops from their shells and scrape off the beard-like fringe and intestinal thread. Cut away the orange flesh. Wash the white parts and pat dry with absorbent kitchen paper. Cut in slices about 5 mm/¼ in thick. Wash and prepare the coral in the same way, if you like. Scrub the scallop shells well and leave to drain. Put the sliced scallops in a bowl and pour over the lemon juice. (There should be enough almost to cover them.) Cover with cling film and put in the refrigerator for 24 hours, stirring occasionally.

When ready to serve, prepare the shallots and herbs. Drain off the lemon juice from the scallops and stir in the oil. Add the shallots and herbs and mix well. Spoon on to the shells and serve immediately with brown bread and butter.

COOK'S TIP

Smooth-skinned lemons are the juiciest. An average lemon yields about 3 tablespoons of juice. To increase the amount of juice, immerse the fruit in boiling water.

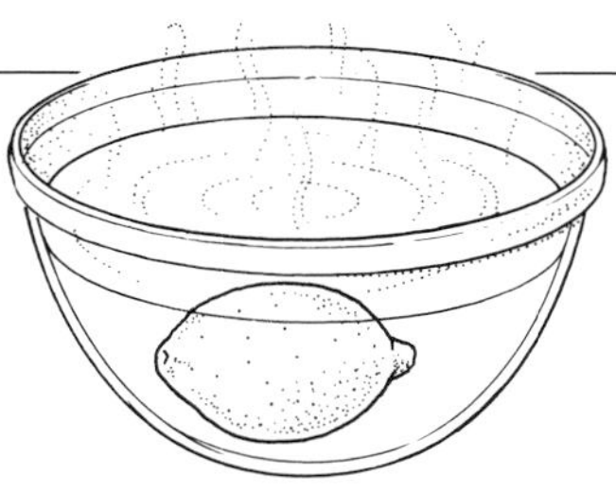

29 PALM HEART SALAD

Preparation time:
30 minutes

Serves 8

Calories:
132 per portion

YOU WILL NEED:
2 x 250 g/9 oz cans palm hearts, drained
500 g/18 oz cooked prawns, unshelled weight
6 tablespoons Mayonnaise (see recipe 219)
4 tablespoons natural yogurt
1 anchovy fillet, pounded
1/4 teaspoon medium hot curry powder
2 tablespoons finely chopped fresh mint
salt and pepper

Cut the palm hearts into thick slices and put in a shallow dish. Shell the prawns and add to the dish. Reserve the heads and shells for stock and use for another recipe.

Mix the mayonnaise with the yogurt, anchovy fillet and curry powder, then pour over the salad.

Toss gently but thoroughly to coat everything with the dressing, then scatter the mint on top and sprinkle with salt and pepper.

COOK'S TIP

Canned palm hearts are obtainable from specialist food shops. They are a true luxury because when these tender shoots are cut off the tree, it dies.

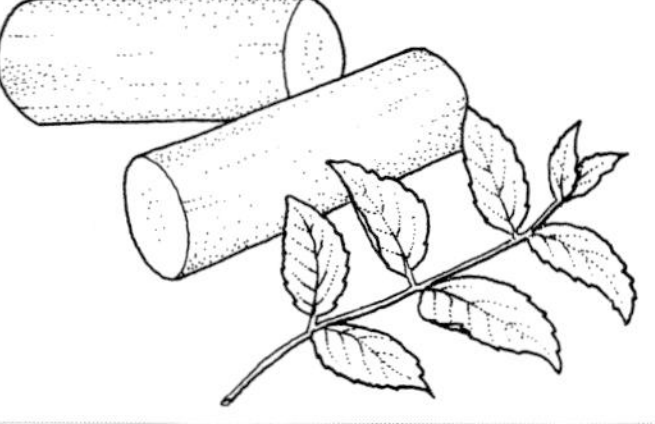

30 PRAWN-STUFFED CUCUMBERS

Preparation time:
20 minutes

Serves 4

Calories:
118 per portion

YOU WILL NEED:
1 large cucumber, cut into 8 pieces
75 g/3 oz cream cheese
2 tablespoons lemon juice
100 g/4 oz peeled, cooked prawns
1 x 100 g/4 oz can pimientos, drained and chopped
8 fresh mint leaves, chopped
salt and pepper
paprika

Hollow out the centre of each cucumber section to form cup shapes and stand upright on a serving dish.

Mix the cream cheese and lemon juice together. Set aside 8 prawns for garnish. Add the remainder to the cheese mixture, with the pimientos and mint. Season with salt, pepper and paprika to taste; mix well.

Pile the filling into the cucumber cups and garnish with the reserved prawns. Serve with thin slices of buttered brown bread.

COOK'S TIP

Before hollowing out each cucumber section, make sure that its ends are straight and not slanted so that it stands level.

31 PRAWNS AND MELON IN DILL SAUCE

Preparation time:
20 minutes, plus chilling

Serves 4

Calories:
207 per portion

YOU WILL NEED:
1 small honeydew melon
225 g/8 oz peeled, cooked prawns
juice of ½ lemon
FOR THE SAUCE
100 g/4 oz medium fat cream cheese
6-8 tablespoons buttermilk
salt and pepper
1 teaspoon dill vinegar or lemon juice
2½ tablespoons chopped fresh dill

Cut the flesh of the melon into small cubes and mix it with the prawns. Sprinkle with the lemon juice.

Purée the cream cheese in a blender with 2 tablespoons of the buttermilk, adding up to 8 tablespoons of buttermilk until the mixture reaches the consistency of medium thick cream. The quantity of buttermilk needed will depend on the consistency of the cheese. Add salt and pepper to taste, the dill vinegar (or lemon juice) and 2 tablespoons of the chopped dill, reserving the rest for garnish.

Mix the sauce with the prawns and melon, and chill for 1 hour before serving. Mix again just before serving, and sprinkle with the remaining dill.

COOK'S TIP

Dill vinegar is available from delicatessens. Alternatively, you can make it by simply putting some sprigs of fresh dill in a bottle and covering with white wine vinegar. Leave for a week, shaking the bottle occasionally.

32 SMOKED TROUT AND ORANGE SALAD

Preparation time:
25 minutes, plus chilling

Serves 4

Calories:
254 per portion

YOU WILL NEED:
350 g/12 oz smoked trout fillets, skinned and boned
½ cucumber, very thinly sliced
3 oranges, peeled, pith removed and segmented
3 celery sticks, trimmed and thinly sliced
FOR THE DRESSING
40 g/1½ oz dessert apple, grated
1 tablespoon lemon juice
3 tablespoons Mayonnaise (see recipe 219)
1½ teaspoons creamed horseradish
FOR THE GARNISH
lettuce leaves
1 bunch watercress
cayenne

To make the dressing, mix the apple with the lemon juice, mayonnaise and creamed horseradish, blending well.

Flake the smoked trout into bite-sized pieces. Place in a bowl with the cucumber, orange segments and celery, tossing gently to mix.

To serve, line a serving dish with a few lettuce leaves. Top with the smoked trout mixture and spoon over the dressing. Chill lightly before serving garnished with sprigs of watercress and sprinkled with cayenne.

COOK'S TIP

It is easier to prepare the orange segments if the fruit is first chilled in the salad drawer of the refrigerator. Use a very sharp knife to remove the peel and pith.

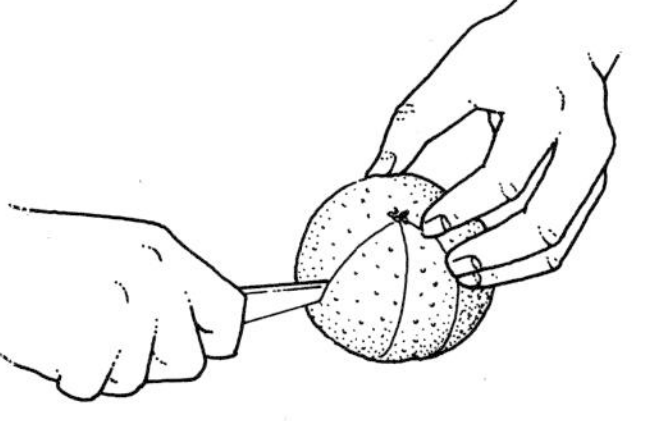

33 MELON AND ANCHOVY SALAD

Preparation time:
15 minutes, plus chilling

Serves 4

Calories:
66 per portion

YOU WILL NEED:
1 melon
1 x 50 g/2 oz can anchovy fillets
juice of 1 lemon
juice of 1 orange
1 teaspoon caster sugar (optional)
watercress sprigs, to garnish

Halve the melon and discard the seeds. Scoop the flesh into a serving dish, using a melon baller or cut into cubes.

Drain the anchovy fillets, reserving 1 tablespoon of the oil. Cut the anchovies into short slivers and add to the melon.

Mix the lemon and orange juice with the reserved anchovy oil and pour over the salad. Add sugar to taste. Chill before serving, garnished with watercress.

COOK'S TIP

A melon baller is an inexpensive gadget, readily available. It can also be used to cut balls of Edam and similar semi-hard cheese.

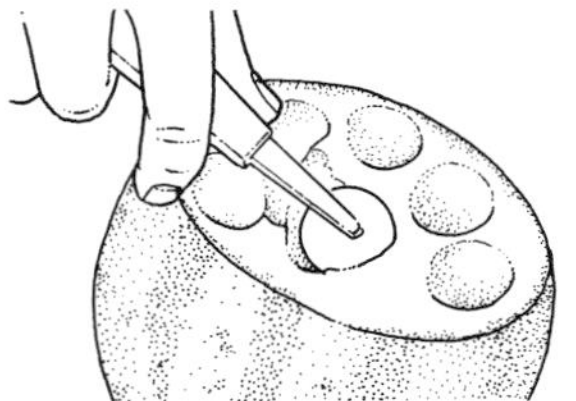

34 MIDDLE EASTERN SALAD

Preparation time:
20 minutes, plus marinating

Cooking time:
1 minute

Serves 4

Calories:
191 per portion

YOU WILL NEED:
1 pitta bread, lightly toasted and cut into 2.5 cm/1 inch squares
1 bunch spring onions, chopped
1 small cucumber peeled and chopped
225 g/8 oz tomatoes, skinned and chopped
1 garlic clove, crushed
1 cos lettuce heart, sliced
50 g/2 oz purslane (tops only) or watercress leaves
4 tablespoons chopped fresh parsley
4 tablespoons chopped fresh mint
salt and pepper
4 tablespoons olive oil
4 tablespoons lemon juice

Arrange the pieces of toasted pitta bread in a salad bowl. Cover with the spring onions, cucumber, tomatoes and garlic. Leave for 10 minutes to allow the bread to absorb the juices, then add the lettuce, purslane or watercress, parsley and mint. Season to taste with salt and pepper.

Combine the oil and lemon juice and pour evenly over the salad. Toss well and serve immediately while the vegetables are still crisp.

COOK'S TIP

It is better to toast the pitta bread under a preheated grill than to use a toaster as it is difficult to time exactly.

35 MINTED GRAPEFRUIT

Preparation time:
20 minutes, plus freezing

Serves 4

Calories:
70 per portion

YOU WILL NEED:
1 tablespoon lemon juice
250 ml/8 fl oz bottle lemonade
2 tablespoons finely chopped fresh mint
2 large grapefruit
2 oranges
4 mint sprigs, to garnish

Mix together the lemon juice, lemonade and chopped mint. Pour into an ice-cube tray or similar shallow container and freeze to the soft stage.

Halve the grapefruit, using a zig-zag cut to give a decorative edge. Remove the flesh from the halves. Peel and segment the oranges, remove the membranes and cut the segments into pieces. Mix with the grapefruit and return to the grapefruit shells.

Pile the lemon ice on top of the citrus fruit and garnish each grapefruit with a sprig of mint.

COOK'S TIP

Use a small sharp, pointed knife to insert at an angle through the skin to the centre of the grapefruit, making each cut the same depth.

36 PEAR WALDORF SALAD

Preparation time:
30 minutes

Serves 4

Calories:
248 per portion

YOU WILL NEED:
1 lettuce, shredded
2 celery sticks, trimmed and chopped
1 red pepper, cored, seeded and sliced
25 g/1 oz walnut halves
75 g/3 oz green grapes, peeled, halved and seeded
1 dessert pear, peeled, cored and sliced
225 g/8 oz smoked chicken, skinned and boned
FOR THE DRESSING
2 tablespoons natural yogurt
2 tablespoons Mayonnaise (see recipe 219)
2 tablespoons grated cucumber
1 teaspoon grated onion
½ teaspoon chopped fresh tarragon
salt and pepper
FOR THE GARNISH
1 dessert pear, cored and sliced
fresh tarragon sprigs

In a large salad bowl, mix the lettuce with the celery, red pepper, walnuts, grapes, pear and smoked chicken.

To make the dressing, mix the yogurt with the mayonnaise, cucumber, onion and tarragon, blending well. Add salt and pepper to taste.

Just before serving, spoon the dressing over the salad ingredients and toss well to mix. Garnish with slices of pear and a few sprigs of fresh tarragon.

COOK'S TIP

The dressing can be made in advance and stored, covered, in the refrigerator for up to 3 days. Stir well to blend before using.

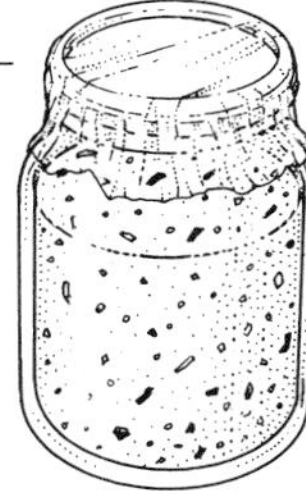

37 HERB AND FLOWER SALAD

Preparation time:
15 minutes

Serves 4

Calories:
96 per portion

YOU WILL NEED:
1 round lettuce, crisp inner leaves only
8 sprigs chervil, torn into small pieces, or 8 leaves sorrel, cut into thin strips
1 handful nasturtium flowers, marigolds or primroses, divided into petals or left whole
FOR THE DRESSING
salt and pepper
½ tablespoon white wine vinegar
½ tablespoon lemon juice
3 tablespoons sunflower oil

Lay the whole lettuce leaves in a salad bowl and scatter with the chervil or sorrel on top. Reserve a few nasturtiums, marigolds or primroses for garnish and scatter the rest over the salad.

To mix the dressing, put salt and pepper in a small bowl and add the vinegar and lemon juice. Stir well, then add the oil and whisk until blended.

Just before serving, pour the dressing over the salad and toss lightly. Scatter the reserved flowers over the top.

COOK'S TIP

Plastic boxes of nasturtium flowers are now available in many large supermarkets but you will probably have to pick the primroses or marigolds in your garden.

38 CELERIAC WITH HERB SAUCE

Preparation time:
20 minutes

Serves 6

Calories:
238 per portion

YOU WILL NEED:
675 g/1½ lb celeriac
FOR THE HERB SAUCE
150 ml/¼ pint mayonnaise (see Cook's Tip)
150 ml/¼ pint natural yogurt
2 hard-boiled egg yolks
1 teaspoon Dijon mustard
salt and pepper
1 tablespoon chopped fresh dill
1 tablespoon chopped chives
1 tablespoon chopped parsley

First, make the herb sauce. Mix the mayonnaise and yogurt together. Mash the egg yolks with the mustard and stir the mayonnaise mixture into them. When smooth, add salt and pepper to taste, then stir in the herbs.

Peel the celeriac and grate it coarsely. Mix it lightly with the herb sauce and transfer to a salad bowl to serve.

COOK'S TIP

The mayonnaise for this sauce need not be home-made; a good commercially prepared mayonnaise will do very well instead.

39 SLIMMER'S DIP

Preparation time:
5 minutes, plus chilling

Serves 4

Calories:
73 per portion

YOU WILL NEED:
1 x 175 g/6 oz can crabmeat
150 ml/¼ piint natural yogurt
salt and pepper
FOR THE GARNISH
lemon slices
parsley sprigs

Combine the crabmeat and the yogurt, seasoning to taste. Place in a small dish and chill. Garnish just before serving with the lemon slices and parsley sprigs.

COOK'S TIP

Serve this dip with 'sticks' or bite-sized pieces of crisp, raw vegetables for a summer-time starter which is very low in calories.

40 GUACAMOLE WITH CRUDITES

Preparation time:
15 minutes

Serves 4

Calories:
271 per portion

YOU WILL NEED:
2 ripe avocados
juice of ½ lemon
2 tomatoes, skinned, seeded and chopped
½ small onion, grated
1 garlic clove, crushed
½ teaspoon Worcestershire sauce
4 tablespoons natural yogurt
salt and pepper
FOR THE CRUDITES
½ small cauliflower
4 carrots
4 celery sticks
½ cucumber
1 green and 1 red pepper, cored and seeded

Halve the avocados and remove the stones. Scoop the flesh into a bowl and mash with the lemon juice. Add the tomatoes, onion, garlic, Worcestershire sauce, yogurt, and salt and pepper to taste. Beat thoroughly until smooth and turn into a serving dish.

Break the cauliflower into florets and cut the remaining vegetables into matchstick pieces.

Place the dish on a large plate and surround with the vegetables.

COOK'S TIP

If this classic Mexican salad dip is not to be served at once, it should be kept in the refrigerator, tightly covered with cling film, to prevent it discolouring.

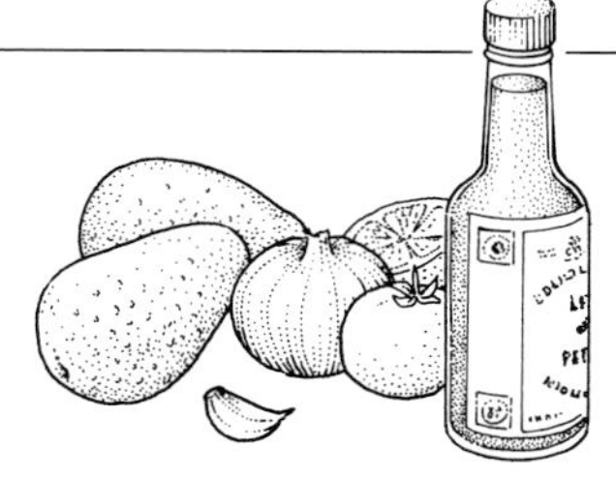

EGG & CHEESE SALADS

Eggs and cheese provide good nutrition and a fine contrast in textures, turning the simplest salads into satisfying and sustaining main course meals.

41 SWEET AND SOUR SALAD

Preparation time:
15 minutes

Serves 4

Calories:
450 per portion

YOU WILL NEED:
1 small curly endive
2 small grapefruit (pink variety, if possible), peeled and segmented
2 small avocados, stoned, peeled and sliced
225 g/8 oz cottage cheese
4 tablespoons sultanas
1 teaspoon grapefruit rind, cut into julienne strips (see Cook's Tip)
50 g/2 oz toasted sesame seeds
FOR THE DRESSING
2 tablespoons lemon juice
1 tablespoon clear honey
6 tablespoons tomato juice
¼ teaspoon mustard powder
salt and pepper

Arrange the largest endive leaves to cover a serving plate and make a 'nest' of the smallest ones in the centre.

Combine the dressing ingredients and toss the grapefruit and avocado in the dressing.

Arrange a ring of alternating grapefruit and avocado slices around the plate on top of the endive. Pour over any remaining dressing.

Mix the cheese with the sultanas and grapefruit rind, pile it in the centre and scatter with sesame seeds.

COOK'S TIP

Julienne strips are matchstick-length strips of peel, cut and trimmed with a sharp knife.

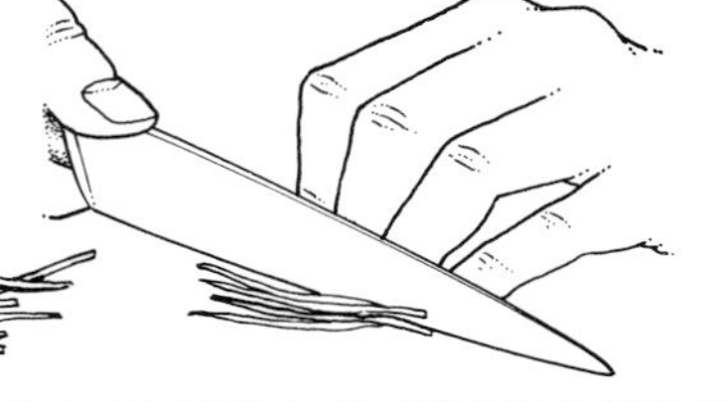

42 GREEK ISLAND SALAD

Preparation time:
20 minutes

Serves 4

Calories:
133 per portion

YOU WILL NEED:
1 small cos lettuce, thinly sliced
½ small cucumber, thinly sliced
2 green peppers, cored, seeded and thinly sliced
1 large onion, thinly sliced into rings
3 large tomatoes, thinly sliced into rings
100 g/4 oz Feta cheese, thinly sliced
salt and pepper
about 4 tablespoons olive oil
2 teaspoons chopped fresh dill, or parsley
sprig of dill or parsley, to garnish

Arrange the salad in layers, in a glass bowl if possible, in the order in which the ingredients are listed, seasoning each layer with a little salt.

Pour half the oil over the tomato layer. Arrange the cheese on top and pour on the remaining oil. Sprinkle on the herb and garnish with a separate sprig.

COOK'S TIP

While this makes an impressive-looking first-course salad, to be served with warm pitta bread, it is also a good salad to serve with main course fish or meat dishes.

43 GREEN SALAD WITH ROQUEFORT CHEESE

Preparation time:
15 minutes

Serves 4

Calories:
134 per portion

YOU WILL NEED:
1 small, curly endive, leaves separated
1 head chicory, leaves torn in half
1 bunch watercress
½ small cucumber, thinly sliced
FOR THE DRESSING
3 tablespoons olive oil
2 teaspoons red wine vinegar
40 g/1½ oz Roquefort cheese, crumbled
freshly ground black pepper
1 tablespoon natural yogurt

Toss together all the salad ingredients and put them into a bowl.

Mix the dressing ingredients well together; pour it over the salad just before serving. Toss well.

COOK'S TIP

Roquefort, a French sheep's cheese, is one of the three great blue cheeses, the others being English Stilton and Gorgonzola from Italy. All three are used in salads and dressings. If Roquefort is not available, Stilton would replace it well in this recipe.

44 WATERCRESS AND SOFT CHEESE SALAD

Preparation time:
20 minutes

Serves 4

Calories:
163 per portion

YOU WILL NEED:
1 bunch watercress
450 g/1 lb tomatoes
4 Petit Suisse cheeses
4 tablespoons chopped chives
salt and pepper
pinch of sugar
½ teaspoon mustard powder
1 tablespoon white wine vinegar
3 tablespoons olive oil

Wash the watercress well and dry on a clean tea-towel. Pick off the tender sprigs of the watercress and lay them around the rims of 4 individual plates. Skin and slice the tomatoes and lay them in the centre of the watercress. Unwrap the Petit Suisse cheeses and roll each one in the chopped chives. Lay them on top of the tomatoes. Sprinkle all over with salt and pepper.

Make a dressing by mixing together the sugar, mustard, vinegar and oil. Serve the dressing separately, or pour over each plate just before serving.

COOK'S TIP

The Petit Suisse cheese can be replaced by any soft cheese, provided it is chilled so that it can be cut into neat pieces before being rolled in the chopped chives.

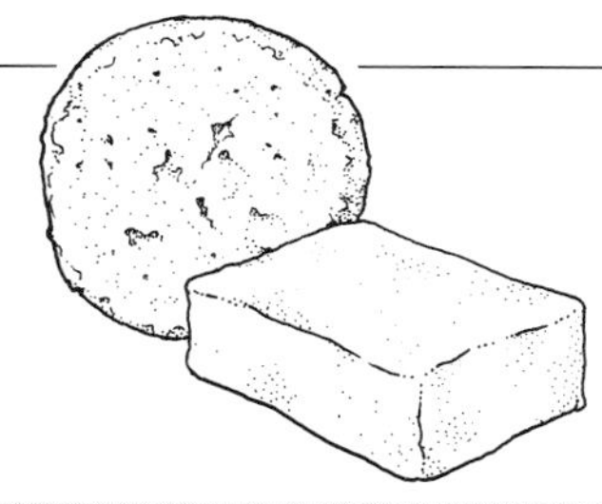

45 APPLE, CELERY AND CHEESE SALAD

Preparation time:
15 minutes

Serves 4

Calories:
376 per portion

YOU WILL NEED:
4 dessert apples, Cox's Orange Pippins preferably
lemon juice
4 celery sticks, trimmed
225 g/8 oz Cheddar cheese
Lemon vinaigrette (see recipe 227), to serve

Core the apples, cut into bite-sized pieces and dip in lemon juice to prevent discoloration. Chop the celery and dice the cheese.

Mix all the ingredients together in a salad bowl. Serve with Lemon vinaigrette.

46 CHEESE AND GRAPE SALAD

Preparation time:
15 minutes

Serves 4

Calories:
293 per portion, plus dressing

YOU WILL NEED:
1 small endive
1 head radicchio
175 g/6 oz semi-hard cheese (e.g. Cheddar, Lancashire, Gruyère)
175 g/6 oz white grapes
salad dressing (see Cook's Tip)

Wash, dry and separate the endive leaves and the radicchio leaves. Cut the cheese into 1 cm/½ inch cubes. Wash and drain the grapes.

Put all the salad ingredients in a salad bowl, add the chosen dressing and toss lightly but thoroughly.

COOK'S TIP

Gruyère cheese can be used instead of Cheddar and 50-70 g/ 2-3 oz chopped walnuts can be added, though the number of calories will then be increased.

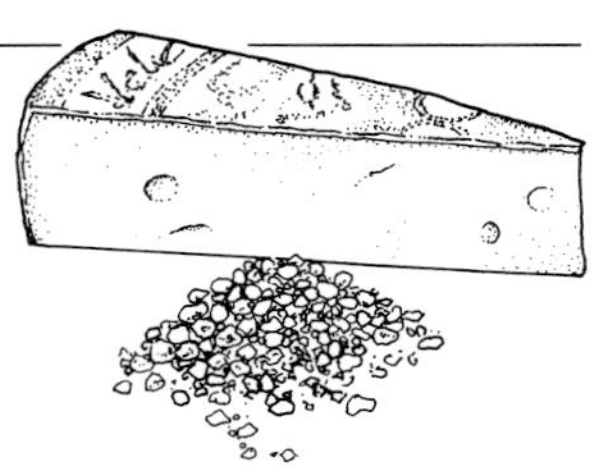

COOK'S TIP

This salad can be simple or exotic, depending on the dressing chosen. Quickest choice is the basic Vinaigrette (recipe 225) made in bulk and stored in the refrigerator.

Green herb dressing (recipe 236) would also be good with this salad.

51 CHEESE, APRICOT AND WALNUT SALAD

Preparation time:
15 minutes

Serves 4

Calories:
186 per portion

YOU WILL NEED:
8 apricots, skinned
4 tablespoons curd or cottage cheese
100 g/4 oz walnuts, chopped
salt and pepper
FOR THE GARNISH
lettuce leaves
2 teaspoons chopped fresh tarragon

Halve the apricots and remove the stones with a small sharp knife.

Mix the curd or cottage cheese with the chopped walnuts, season to taste with salt and pepper, then spoon into the hollows of the apricots.

Arrange the apricots on lettuce leaves and sprinkle with the chopped tarragon. Serve with Orange vinaigrette (see recipe 227).

COOK'S TIP

Walnuts have a tendency to become rancid quite quickly so it is important to check their 'sell by' date. They should be stored in glass or plastic, not metal, containers.

52 ARTICHOKE AND COTTAGE CHEESE SALAD

Preparation time:
10 minutes

Serves 4

Calories:
108 per portion

YOU WILL NEED:
350 g/12 oz cottage cheese
1 small onion, finely grated
salt and pepper
1 x 400 g/14 oz can artichoke hearts
4 tablespoons natural yogurt
4 tablespoons lemon juice
2 tablespoons finely chopped parsley
4 lemon slices, to garnish

Mix the cottage cheese with the grated onion and season to taste. Divide the mixture between 4 individual serving dishes and pile into the centre of each. Drain the artichoke hearts and cut them into quarters. Arrange around the mounds of cottage cheese.

Mix the yogurt with the lemon juice and parsley, season to taste and spoon over the cottage cheese. Garnish each dish with a twist of lemon.

COOK'S TIP

The cottage cheese should be drained before mixing it with the onion as the whey would otherwise spoil the appearance of this salad.

53 CHEESE WITH PRAWNS AND ASPARAGUS

Preparation time:
10 minutes

Serves 4

Calories:
185 per portion

YOU WILL NEED:
450 g/1 lb cottage cheese
225 g/8 oz peeled, cooked prawns
salt and pepper
1 cucumber, peeled and diced
1 x 225 g/8 oz can asparagus spears, drained and chopped
lettuce leaves

Place the cottage cheese and prawns in a bowl and mix together. Add salt and pepper to taste. Stir in the diced cucumber and chopped asparagus.

Make a bed of lettuce leaves on 4 plates. Divide the mixture equally and spoon on to the lettuce.

COOK'S TIP

At the peak of the season when the price is lower, fresh asparagus can be cooked and used instead of canned. Its flavour is superior.

54 EGG AND CHEESE SALAD BOWL

Preparation time:
20 minutes

Serves 4

Calories:
272 per portion

YOU WILL NEED:
4 hard-boiled eggs
1 green pepper, cored, seeded and chopped
100 g/4 oz Edam cheese, cubed
4 celery sticks, roughly chopped
100 g/4 oz raisins
lettuce leaves
2 dessert apples, cored, sliced and dipped in lemon juice

Cut the eggs into quarters and gently mix with the green pepper, cheese, celery and raisins.

Line a salad bowl with lettuce leaves and spoon in the egg mixture. Arrange the apple slices decoratively on top. Serve a bowl of mayonnaise separately.

COOK'S TIP

Cox's Orange Pippins and Granny Smiths are both suitable varieties of apple to use in this salad. If you prefer a rather sharper flavour, choose Granny Smiths.

55 SUNKISSED SALAD

Preparation time:
15 minutes, plus cooling

Cooking time:
10-15 minutes

Serves 4

Calories:
366 per portion

YOU WILL NEED:
450 g/1 lb French beans, trimmed
450 g/1 lb cottage cheese
6 hard-boiled eggs
2 red peppers, cored, seeded and sliced
4 tablespoons French dressing (see recipe 233)

Cook the beans in boiling salted water until tender – about 10-15 minutes. Cool, then arrange on a large round serving dish.

Cut the hard-boiled eggs into quarters. Pile the cottage cheese in the centre of the beans and surround with the quartered hard-boiled eggs. Garnish with the slices of red pepper, between the eggs and around the cottage cheese. Just before serving pour the dressing over the beans and slices of red pepper.

COOK'S TIP

The cooking time for the French beans depends on their size and your personal taste. They are best when used slightly al dente.

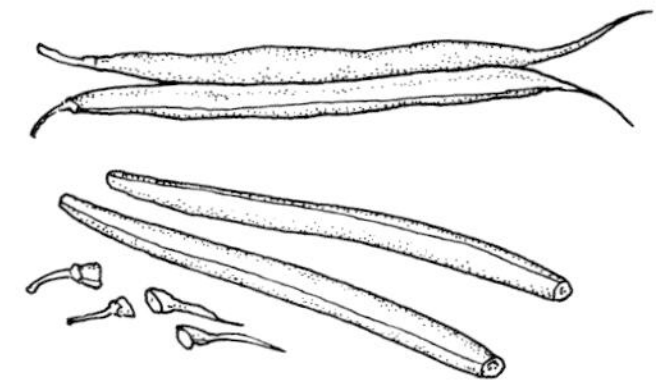

56 FUNNY FACE SALAD

Preparation time:
20 minutes

Serves 4

Calories:
88 per portion

YOU WILL NEED:
1 lettuce
4 eggs, hard-boiled
1 carrot
2 radishes
2 small gherkins
1 celery stick

Shred the lettuce and use to line 4 individual plates.

Halve the hard-boiled eggs and divide between the plates, cut side down.

Garnish each egg with a piece of carrot, half a radish slice, pieces of gherkin and celery curls to represent the nose, mouth, eyes and hair of funny face.

COOK'S TIP

This is an attractive salad for children. If the vegetables are prepared first and the sharp knife put away, even quite small children can safely be allowed to add the 'features' to each funny face. The preparation time will of course be longer!

57 POTATO AND EGG MAYONNAISE

Preparation time:
15 minutes, plus cooling

Cooking time:
15-20 minutes

Serves 4

Calories:
327 per portion

YOU WILL NEED:
450 g/1 lb waxy (salad) potatoes
salt
2 tablespoons French dressing (see recipe 233)
4 spring onions, sliced
4 hard-boiled eggs, chopped
2 dill pickles, chopped
3 tablespoons mayonnaise
3 tablespoons natural yogurt
1 tablespoon chopped fresh fennel, to garnish

Cook the potatoes in their skins in boiling salted water for 15-20 minutes until tender. Drain well, chop roughly and place in a bowl. Pour over the French dressing while still warm, toss thoroughly and leave to cool. Add the spring onions, chopped eggs and dill pickles.

Mix together the mayonnaise, yogurt and 2 tablespoons juice from the dill pickles until smooth. Pour over the salad and mix thoroughly. Transfer to a shallow dish and sprinkle with the fennel to serve.

COOK'S TIP

Try making a Swedish version of potato salad. Omit the hard-boiled eggs from the above recipe and add 100 g/4 oz chopped cooked beetroot.

58 SORREL, EGG AND POTATO SALAD

Preparation time:
15 minutes, plus cooling

Cooking time:
15-20 minutes

Serves 4

Calories:
254 per portion

YOU WILL NEED:
1 round lettuce
225 g/8 oz new potatoes
4 tablespoons olive oil
4 hard-boiled eggs
4 tablespoons shredded sorrel
salt and pepper
pinch of sugar
½ teaspoon French mustard
1 tablespoon white wine vinegar

Tear the lettuce into pieces and place in a salad bowl. Boil the potatoes in their skins. Peel and slice them thickly as soon as they are cool enough to handle. Pour 1 tablespoon of the olive oil over them while they are still hot.

Slice the eggs thickly. When the potatoes have cooled, pile them in the centre of the lettuce and surround with the sliced eggs. Scatter the shredded sorrel over the salad.

Make a dressing with salt and pepper, sugar, mustard, vinegar and the remaining oil. Pour over the salad just before serving.

COOK'S TIP

If sorrel is unavailable, substitute salad spinach leaves which are sold prepared ready to eat in some supermarkets, particularly in the early summer.

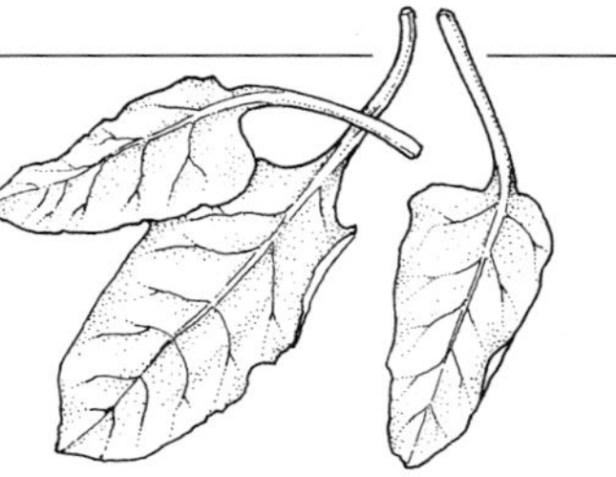

59 EGGS MIMOSA

Preparation time:
10 minutes

Serves 4

Calories:
272 per portion

YOU WILL NEED:
4 hard-boiled eggs
40 g/1 ½ oz keta
6 tablespoons Mayonnaise (see recipe 219)
1 small lettuce, to garnish

Halve the eggs lengthways, remove the yolks and arrange the whites in a serving dish. Fill the egg white hollows with the caviar, reserving 1 tablespoon for garnish. Spoon the mayonnaise over the eggs, covering them completely.

Garnish with the reserved egg yolk and lettuce. Serve with thin slices of brown bread.

COOK'S TIP

For a less rich mixture, replace the keta (salmon roe) with 100 g/4 oz lumpfish roe, and the mayonnaise with 150 ml/¼ pint natural yogurt and the juice of 1 lemon, seasoned to taste with salt and pepper.

60 SARDINE EGGS

Preparation time:
15 minutes

Serves 4

Calories:
208 per portion

YOU WILL NEED:
4 hard-boiled eggs
1 x 100 g/4 oz can sardines in oil
1 tablespoon fresh white breadcrumbs
2 tablespoons Mayonnaise (see recipe 219)
1 tablespoon lemon juice
salt and pepper
chopped parsley, to garnish

Cut the eggs in half lengthways and remove the yolks. Drain the sardines, discard any bones and chop finely.

Mash the egg yolks, then mix with the sardines, breadcrumbs, mayonnaise and lemon juice. Season with salt and pepper to taste and beat until thoroughly blended. Pile the mixture into the egg white halves.

Garnish with chopped parsley and serve with buttered wholemeal bread.

COOK'S TIP

For special occasions pipe the sardine mixture decoratively into the egg white halves, using a medium star tube in a nylon piping bag.

61 JERUSALEM ARTICHOKE SALAD

Preparation time:
20 minutes, plus cooling

Cooking time:
10-15 minutes

Serves 4

Calories:
110 per portion

YOU WILL NEED:
450 g/1 lb Jerusalem artichokes
lettuce leaves
wine vinegar
pinch of ground mace
4 hard-boiled eggs

Peel the Jerusalem artichokes and boil for 10-15 minutes until tender. Drain and allow to cool. Cut in slices.

Line a salad bowl with lettuce leaves. Arrange the sliced artichokes on top of the lettuce. Sprinkle with a little vinegar to keep them white. Add the mace.

Sieve the egg yolks and chop the whites, then scatter over the lettuce and artichokes. Serve with Lemon or Orange vinaigrette (see recipe 227).

COOK'S TIP

Cook a few extra Jerusalem artichokes and use small pieces in a dish of sauced scallops. The artichokes absorb the flavour of the sauce well.

62 EGG AND CUCUMBER SALAD

Preparation time:
15 minutes

Serves 4

Calories:
134 per portion

YOU WILL NEED:
1 bunch watercress
1 cucumber, peeled and sliced
4 hard-boiled eggs, finely chopped
1 bunch spring onions, chopped
FOR THE SAUCE
300 ml/½ pint natural yogurt
1 tablespoon lemon juice
1 teaspoon mustard powder
salt and pepper

Arrange the watercress in a serving dish and cover with the cucumber slices. Mix the chopped eggs and spring onions together and spoon into the centre.

To make the sauce, mix all the ingredients together. Pour over the salad and serve.

COOK'S TIP

Pick over the watercress carefully and reserve the thicker stems to add to soups. When seasoning the sauce remember that watercress has quite a peppery taste.

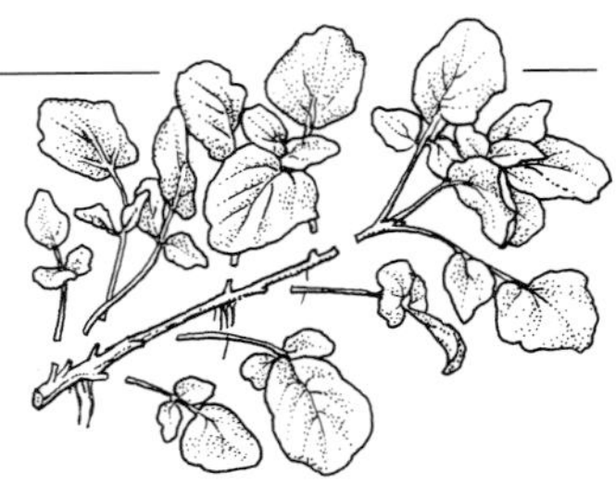

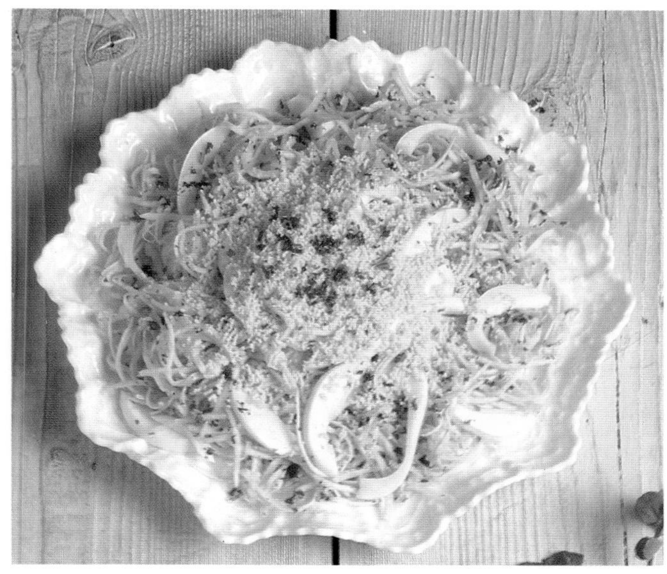

63 CELERIAC AND EGG SALAD

Preparation time:
15 minutes, plus standing

Serves 4

Calories:
253 per portion

YOU WILL NEED:
450 g/1 lb celeriac
6 tablespoons French dressing (see recipe 233)
2 hard-boiled eggs
1 tablespoon chopped parsley

Grate the celeriac finely and place in a mixing bowl. Pour over the dressing, toss thoroughly and leave for 1 hour.

Shred the egg whites finely and mix with the celeriac. Place in a shallow serving dish and sieve the egg yolks over the top. Sprinkle with the parsley to serve.

64 CURRIED EGG SALAD

Preparation time:
10 minutes

Serves 4

Calories:
439 per portion

YOU WILL NEED:
150 ml/¼ pint Mayonnaise (see recipe 219)
4 tablespoons double cream
about 1 tablespoon curry paste
salt and pepper
6 hard-boiled eggs
1 crisp lettuce
salad cress or watercress, to garnish

Mix together the mayonnaise, cream and curry paste. Season with salt and pepper to taste. Cut the eggs into quarters and carefully fold into the mayonnaise mixture until they are evenly coated.

Line a serving dish with the lettuce leaves. Pile the egg mixture in the centre and garnish with cress or watercress.

COOK'S TIP

The uneven surface of celeriac makes it difficult to peel. If the root is first cut in thick slices, it is easier to remove the peel.

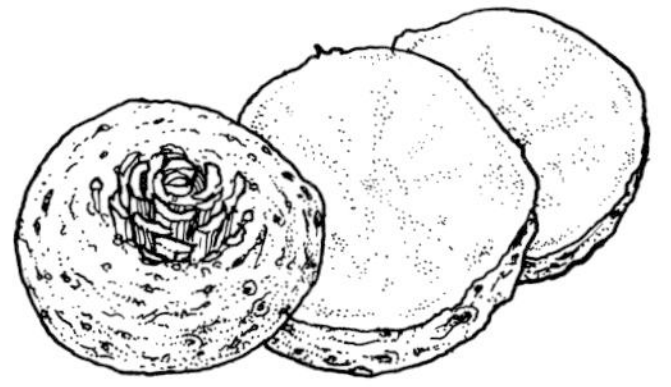

COOK'S TIP

The amount of curry paste depends on your personal preferences. For a less rich sauce replace the cream with natural yogurt.

WORLD CHOICE

Here are deliciously different salads from Europe, the Middle East, South-East Asia, the Far East and the Americas. Their ingredients and flavourings, though often exotic and unusual, are all readily available in our shops and supermarkets – so it is easy to bring an international touch to all kinds of meal.

65 SALAD NIÇOISE

Preparation time:
20 minutes

Serves 4

Calories:
367 per portion

YOU WILL NEED:
1 large crisp lettuce or ½ curly endive or 2 heads radicchio
225 g/8 oz firm tomatoes, quartered
225 g/8 oz new potatoes, steamed and cooled
175 g/6 oz stringless green beans, topped, tailed, steamed and cooled
4 hard-boiled eggs, quartered
1 x 90 g/3½ oz can tuna fish, drained and flaked
8 anchovy fillets
50 g/2 oz black olives
FOR THE DRESSING
6 tablespoons olive oil
2 tablespoons red wine vinegar
1 teaspoon French mustard
salt and pepper

Tear the lettuce, endive or radicchio into even-sized pieces and arrange in a shallow salad bowl or on a large flat serving dish. Arrange the other ingredients attractively on top.

Thoroughly combine all the dressing ingredients in a jug. Pour a little of the dressing over the salad just before serving and hand the remainder separately.

COOK'S TIP

In Nice a bowl of Aïoli (see recipe 235) often accompanies this salad. The vegetables can be varied according to what is in season: for example, lightly cooked cauliflower florets, raw carrot slivers and mangetout.

66 TUSCAN SALAD

Preparation time:
25-30 minutes

Serves 4

Calories:
663 per portion

YOU WILL NEED:
4 new potatoes, boiled in their skins
4 tablespoons mayonnaise
1 tablespoon chopped parsley
1 x 400 g/14 oz can artichoke hearts
1 x 400 g/14 oz can flageolet or cannellini beans, drained
1 x 100 g/4 oz can sardines, drained
50 g/2 oz salami or garlic sausage, rindless and rolled into cornets
2 hard-boiled eggs, quartered
8 cherry tomatoes
50 g/2 oz canned anchovy fillets
FOR THE DRESSING
3 tablespoons red wine vinegar
1 tablespoon lemon juice
1 small garlic clove, crushed
1½ teaspoons wholegrain mustard
8 tablespoons olive oil
salt and pepper

To make the dressing, beat the vinegar with the lemon juice, garlic and mustard. Gradually add the oil to make a thickened dressing. Add salt and pepper to taste.

Slice the potatoes and mix with the mayonnaise and parsley. Arrange the artichoke hearts, beans, sardines, sausage, eggs and potato salad around the edge of a large platter.

Cut a cross in the top of each tomato and open out slightly. Place the tomatoes in the centre of the platter and cover with a lattice of anchovy. Drizzle over the dressing.

COOK'S TIP

Cherry tomatoes are miniature in size with a sweet taste. They should have a bright red skin and be firm to the touch.

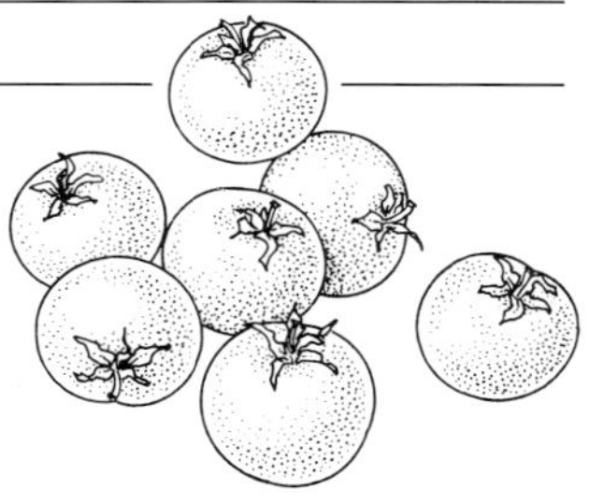

67 SCANDINAVIAN PICKLED HERRING SALAD

Preparation time:
15 minutes

Serves 4

Calories:
290 per portion

YOU WILL NEED:
1 x 350 ml/12 fl oz jar pickled herrings, drained
3 pickled dill cucumbers, thinly sliced
2 red dessert apples, cored and sliced
1 bunch spring onions, trimmed and chopped
150 ml/¼ pint soured cream
½ teaspoon dried dill

Cut the herrings into thin strips and place in a bowl. Add the sliced dill cucumbers, apples, spring onions, soured cream and dill. Toss well to mix and spoon into a chilled serving dish.

COOK'S TIP

To pickle herrings, lay the cleaned fish in an ovenproof dish and cover with a mixture of three parts wine vinegar and one part water. Add bay leaves, cloves, mace and salt to taste. Cook, covered, for 3-4 hours at 140 C/275 F/ Gas 1.

68 NORWEGIAN MACKEREL SALAD

Preparation time:
10 minutes, plus cooling

Cooking time:
15 minutes

Serves 4

Calories:
214 per portion

YOU WILL NEED:
4 x 75 g/3 oz mackerel fillets
4 x 100 g/4 oz boiled potatoes, sliced
lettuce leaves
4 tomatoes, sliced
FOR THE MUSTARD SAUCE
4 tablespoons mayonnaise
4 teaspoons French or English made mustard
salt and pepper

Place the mackerel under a preheated hot grill and cook for about 15 minutes, turning occasionally. Leave to cool, then remove the skin with a sharp knife.

Divide the flesh into pieces and arrange on 4 plates. Place some potato slices on one side of each plate. On the other side, place some lettuce leaves and tomato slices.

Mix the mayonnaise, mustard, salt and pepper together. Serve the sauce separately or pour over the mackerel.

COOK'S TIP

If serving the sauce separately, sprinkle the mackerel with coarsely ground black pepper. Try using one of the wholegrain mustards in the sauce to vary its texture.

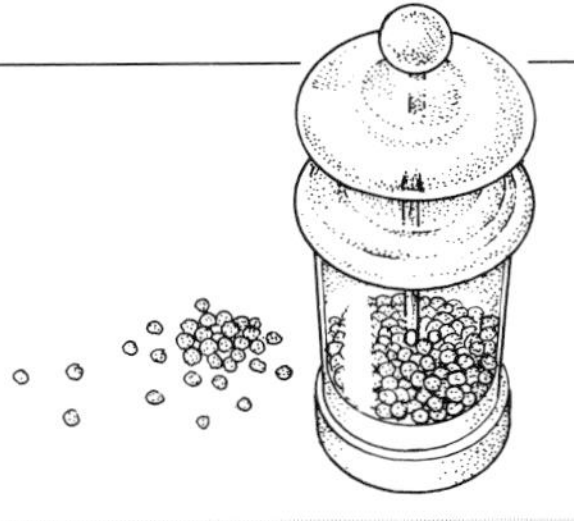

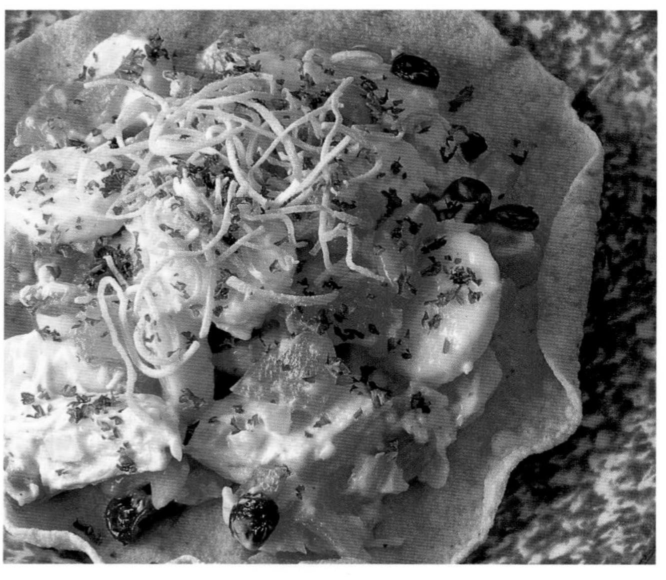

69 MADRAS CHICKEN SALAD

Preparation time:
25 minutes, plus chilling

Serves 4

Calories:
391 per portion

YOU WILL NEED:
350 g/12 oz cooked chicken meat, skinned and boned
2 bananas, sliced
1 tablespoon lemon juice
50 g/2 oz cashew nuts (salted or unsalted)
25 g/1 oz raisins
50 g/2 oz dried apricots, coarsely chopped
1 tablespoon long-thread coconut, toasted for garnish
FOR THE DRESSING
3 tablespoons mayonnaise
1 tablespoon finely chopped onion
½ teaspoon hot Madras curry powder
½ teaspoon lemon juice
2 tablespoons grated dessert apple
1 teaspoon mango chutney
pinch of salt

To make the dressing, mix the mayonnaise with the other ingredients, blending well.

Cut the chicken into bite-sized pieces. Place in a serving bowl with the bananas and lemon juice, tossing gently to mix. Add the cashew nuts, raisins and dried apricots, blending well.

Just before serving, spoon the dressing over the salad ingredients and toss well to mix. Chill lightly before serving sprinkled with the toasted coconut.

COOK'S TIP

For special occasions, serve this salad on bought plain or spiced poppadums and drink iced lager.

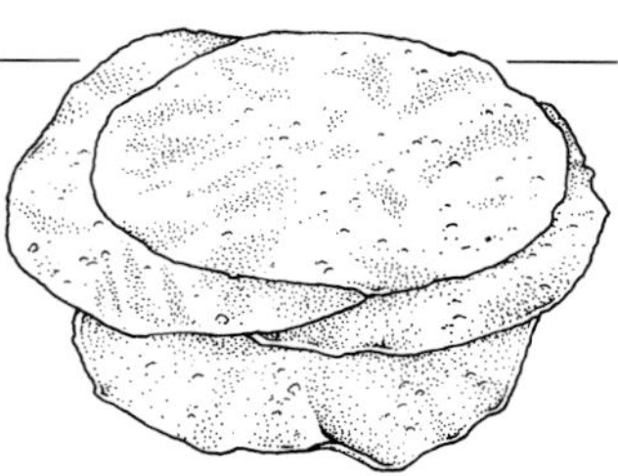

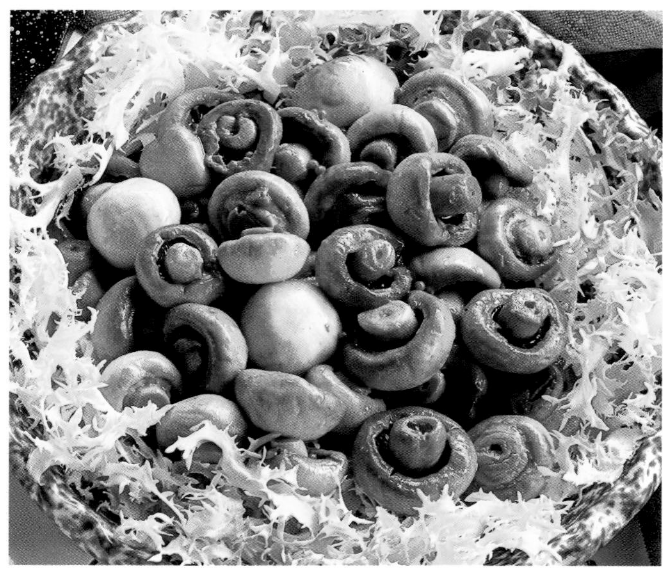

70 MUSHROOMS A LA GRECQUE

Preparation time:
5 minutes, plus cooling

Cooking time:
5 minutes

Serves 4

Calories:
93 per portion

YOU WILL NEED:
2 tablespoons lemon juice
2 tablespoons olive oil
150 ml/¼ pint dry white wine
1 teaspoon coriander seeds
1 sprig parsley
1 sprig fresh thyme
1 small celery stalk with leaves
1 bay leaf
12 black peppercorns
225 g/8 oz button mushrooms, washed, unpeeled
½ head curly endive

Combine all the ingredients except the mushrooms and curly endive in a small saucepan and bring to the boil. Add the mushrooms to the pan and simmer for 5 minutes over a gentle heat. Remove from the heat, cover and leave to cool completely in the liquid – about 2-3 hours.

Discard the parsley, thyme, celery stalk and bay leaf. Arrange a bed of curly endive leaves in a shallow serving dish. Spoon the mushrooms and the liquid into the centre.

COOK'S TIP

This mushroom salad makes a good starter before a fish main course. Serve plenty of hot crusty French bread to mop up the delicious juices.

71 RATATOUILLE

Preparation time:
25 minutes, plus standing

Cooking time:
about 30 minutes

Serves 6

Calories:
243 per portion

YOU WILL NEED:
2 aubergines
salt and pepper
about 150 ml/¼ pint sunflower oil
1 Spanish onion, finely chopped
1 green pepper, cored, seeded and chopped
1 red pepper, cored, seeded and chopped
225 g/8 oz small courgettes, unpeeled and sliced
225 g/8 oz tomatoes, skinned and chopped
2 garlic cloves, crushed
3 tablespoons chopped fresh basil

Cut the unpeeled aubergines into cubes and sprinkle with salt; leave for 20 minutes to drain.

Heat the oil in a wide heavy-based pan. Cook the onion gently for about 6 minutes. Pat the aubergine dry with absorbent kitchen paper and add it to the onion with the peppers. Cook gently, adding more oil as necessary, for 10 minutes, then add the courgettes and cook for a further 5 minutes. Finally add the tomatoes and the garlic and cook for 10 minutes more until all is soft and slightly mushy. Add plenty of salt and pepper and stir in the chopped basil.

COOK'S TIP

Ratatouille is equally good served hot or cold. If serving hot, leave for 4-5 minutes after adding the basil to allow the flavour to permeate the mixture.

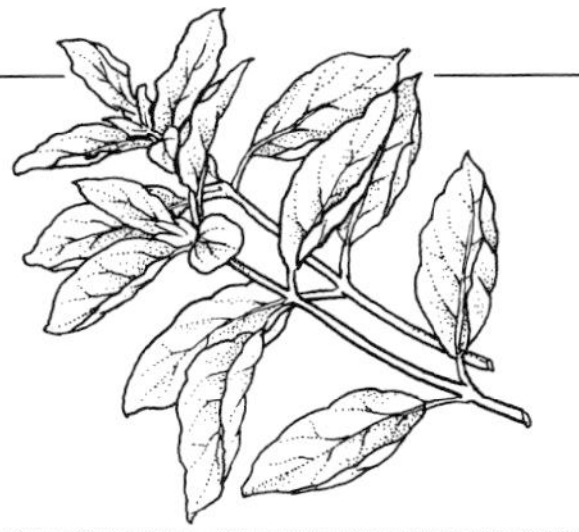

72 SAUERKRAUT

Preparation time:
15 minutes, plus standing and cooling

Cooking time:
15-20 minutes

Serves 4

Calories:
74 per portion

YOU WILL NEED:
1 red cabbage, finely shredded
handful of cooking salt
2 tablespoons lemon juice
1 large onion, finely chopped
1 tablespoon olive oil
12 peppercorns
1 bay leaf
1 teaspoon caraway seeds
grated rind of ½ lemon
2 tablespoons vinegar
2 teaspoons soft light brown sugar
250 ml/8 fl oz white stock

Place the cabbage in a large bowl and sprinkle over the salt and the lemon juice. Mix well together, then cover with a small plate and weight it down to press the cabbage. Leave for 1 hour, then squeeze the cabbage with your hands to remove any excess juice and until the cabbage has reduced to half its original bulk. Wash the cabbage under running cold water and squeeze again.

Sauté the onion in the oil until golden. Add the cabbage and cook for 10 minutes. Add the peppercorns, bay leaf, caraway seeds, lemon rind, vinegar, sugar and stock. Sauté together until the cabbage is tender, adding more stock if necessary. Leave to cool.

COOK'S TIP

Sauerkraut can also be served hot as an accompaniment for roast poultry or grilled meat. The pungent caraway seeds give the mixture its distinctive flavour.

73 ORIENTAL VEGETABLES

Preparation time:
10 minutes, plus cooling

Cooking time:
15-20 minutes

Serves 4

Calories:
27 per portion

YOU WILL NEED:
450 g/1 lb mixed vegetables: cauliflower, onions, mushrooms, leeks and fennel
1 wine glass white wine
1 wine glass wine vinegar
1 teaspoon ground coriander
1 teaspoon ground mace
1 teaspoon dried rosemary
salt
soft light brown sugar (optional)

Cut the cauliflower into florets, the onions into quarters or eighths depending on size, the leeks and fennel into slices. Leave the mushrooms whole.

Place all the vegetables in a saucepan with the white wine, vinegar, spices, rosemary and salt. Add enough water to cover, bring to the boil and simmer gently for 15-20 minutes. The vegetables should be slightly crisp.

When cooked, taste, and if very sharp add sugar to taste. Leave to cool.

COOK'S TIP

Other combinations of vegetables can be used but those given above are good for a winter salad. The vegetables can also be served hot.

74 SWEET 'N' SOUR SALAD

Preparation time:
15 minutes

Serves 4

Calories:
101 per portion

YOU WILL NEED:
100 g/4 oz mushrooms, sliced
6 spring onions, chopped
100 g/4 oz beansprouts
50 g/2 oz bambooshoots, sliced
225 g/8 oz Chinese leaves, coarsely shredded
FOR THE DRESSING
2 tablespoons corn oil
1 tablespoon clear honey
1 tablespoon soy sauce
2 tablespoons lemon juice

Make the dressing: combine the oil, honey, soy sauce and lemon juice in a large bowl and mix until well blended.

Add the mushrooms to the dressing and stir until they are well coated. Stir in the spring onions, beansprouts and bamboo shoots. Add the Chinese leaves and toss well. Transfer to a glass salad bowl to serve.

COOK'S TIP

This makes a good side salad for serving with pork – either chops, spare ribs or slices of cold roast pork. Chopped apple is a useful addition to the salad.

75 FAR EAST SALAD

Preparation time:
15 minutes, plus marinating

Serves 4

Calories:
118 per portion

YOU WILL NEED:
225 g/8 oz spring greens, very finely shredded
4 tablespoons Shoyu dressing (see recipe 234)
3 celery sticks, sliced
4 spring onions, chopped
1 red pepper, cored, seeded and diced

Place the spring greens in a bowl with the dressing, toss thoroughly and leave to marinate for 1 hour. Add the remaining ingredients and toss thoroughly. Transfer to a salad bowl to serve.

COOK'S TIP

Shoyu is naturally fermented soy sauce, made from soya beans with wheat or barley. Since shoyu is quite salty and well flavoured there is no need to add extra salt or pepper in this recipe.

76 ORIENTAL MANGETOUT

Preparation time:
15 minutes, plus soaking

Cooking time:
4-5 minutes

Serves 4

Calories:
191 per portion

YOU WILL NEED:
3-4 Chinese dried mushrooms
4 tablespoons vegetable oil
50 g/2 oz bamboos hoots, sliced
50 g/2 oz beansprouts
1 tablespoon caster sugar
1 tablespoon light soy sauce
2 teaspoons salt
50 g/2 oz button mushrooms
50 g/2 oz mangetout peas
50 g/2 oz broccoli, chopped
1 small carrot, chopped
1 tablespoon cornflour
2 tablespoons water
2 teaspoons sesame seed oil

Soak the dried mushrooms in cold water for about 30-40 minutes. Squeeze dry and discard the stalks.

Heat half the oil in a wok or frying pan, add the soaked mushrooms, bamboo shoots and beansprouts and stir-fry for 1 minute. Add the sugar, soy sauce and half the salt, stir for a few seconds, then remove with a slotted spoon and set aside on a plate.

Wipe the wok with absorbent kitchen paper and heat the remaining oil. Add the remaining vegetables and salt and stir-fry for about 2 minutes. Mix in the dried mushrooms, bamboo shoots and beansprouts and stir-fry for a few seconds. Blend the cornflour with the water to make a smooth paste and stir into the wok. Add the oil, stir well to mix and pile on to a heated serving dish.

COOK'S TIP

This warm Oriental salad becomes a light main course dish if served topped with a freshly made omelette cut into strips.

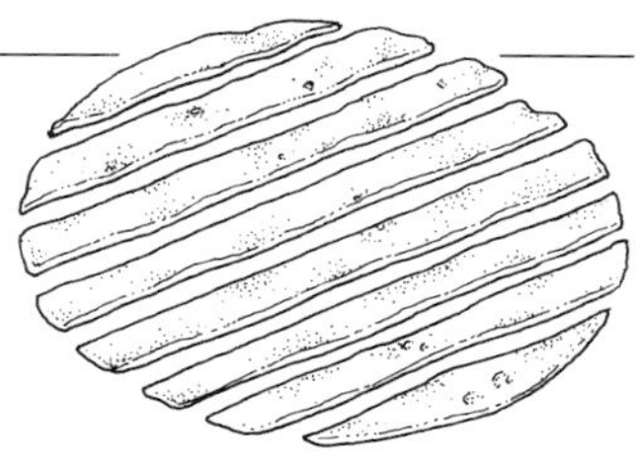

77 MEDITERRANEAN MIXED SALAD

Preparation time:
15-20 minutes

Serves 4

Calories:
100 per portion

YOU WILL NEED:
50 g/2 oz rocket, shredded
1 bunch spring onions, thinly sliced
½ cucumber, peeled and chopped
1 green pepper, cored, seeded and chopped
2 tablespoons chopped fresh dill
FOR THE DRESSING
1 tablespoon lemon juice
2½ tablespoons olive oil

Pile the shredded rocket into a salad bowl, and scatter the remaining ingredients over it.

Combine the dressing ingredients in a small jug and pour over the salad and mix thoroughly. Serve with simple dishes of grilled meat or fish.

78 CONTINENTAL MIXED SALAD

Preparation time:
15 minutes

Serves 4-6

Calories:
109-73 per portion

YOU WILL NEED:
½ head endive, trimmed
1 large head chicory, trimmed
1 head radicchio
1 bunch watercress, trimmed
FOR THE DRESSING
3-4 tablespoons olive oil
¼ teaspoon salt
pinch of pepper
pinch of caster sugar
½ teaspoon French mustard
1 tablespoon wine vinegar

Separate the endive leaves and place in a salad bowl. Slice the chicory crossways into thin rings and add to the endive. Separate the radicchio leaves and add to the salad bowl. Add the watercress.

Place all the dressing ingredients in a screw-top jar and shake well to blend thoroughly.

Just before serving, pour the dressing over the salad and toss until all the leaves are well coated.

COOK'S TIP

Rocket has a slightly bitter, peppery taste and was popular in Tudor times. It must be washed thoroughly as it can be gritty. Discard the coarser stalks and leaves.

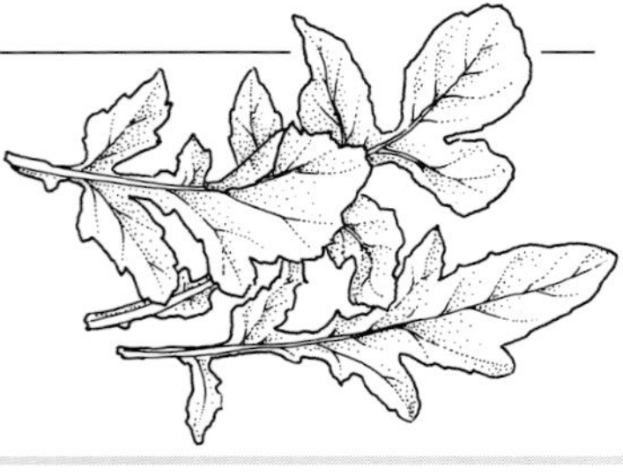

COOK'S TIP

Variations on this basic salad could include corn salad (mâche) instead of the watercress and crisp Webb's lettuce for the curly endive. Diced cucumber and tomato, and thin slices of onion make good additions.

79 FRENCH-STYLE CELERIAC

Preparation time:
10 minutes

Serves 4

Calories:
107 per portion

YOU WILL NEED:
1 large celeriac, cut into matchstick strips
salt
2-3 tablespoons thick Mayonnaise (see recipe 219)
¼ teaspoon French mustard
FOR THE GARNISH
chopped fresh parsley
a little paprika

Blanch the celeriac in a saucepan of boiling salted water for 2-3 minutes or until just tender. Drain thoroughly and allow to cool.

Blend the mayonnaise with the mustard in a salad bowl. Add the celeriac and toss well. Sprinkle with the parsley and paprika and serve immediately.

COOK'S TIP

To turn this salad into a main dish, add small strips of cooked chicken or turkey to the mayonnaise mixture with the celeriac.

80 SWEDISH POTATO SALAD

Preparation time:
15 minutes, plus cooling

Cooking time:
15-20 minutes

Serves 6

Calories:
141 per portion

YOU WILL NEED:
675 g/1½ lb small new potatoes
salt
2 tablespoons French dressing (see recipe 233)
100 g/4 oz cooked beetroot, diced
1 pickled dill cucumber, diced
5 tablespoons Yogurt dressing (see recipe 240)
1 tablespoon chopped fresh dill

Scrub the potatoes to remove any earth but leave the skins on. Cook in boiling salted water until tender. Drain and mix with the French dressing while still warm. Leave to cool.

Add the diced beetroot and cucumber with the yogurt dressing. Mix well, then transfer to a salad bowl. Sprinkle with the dill before serving.

COOK'S TIP

Use a glass or china bowl for this salad as the beetroot juice would stain a wooden bowl. For the same reason do not use wooden salad servers.

81 GADO-GADO SALAD

Preparation time:
30 minutes, plus standing

Cooking time:
25-30 minutes

Serves 6

Calories:
617 per portion

YOU WILL NEED:
225 g/8 oz green beans, halved
225 g/8 oz white cabbage, shredded
225 g/8 oz carrots, finely sliced
225 g /8 oz waxy potatoes, diced
225 g/8 oz beansprouts
1 cucumber, quartered and sliced
2 hard-boiled eggs, sliced
225 g/8 oz desiccated coconut
450 ml/¾ pint boiling water
5 fresh chillies, seeded
3 garlic cloves, crushed
1 teaspoon blachan (see Cook's Tip)
225 g/8 oz crunchy peanut butter
2.5 cm/1 inch piece root ginger, grated
2 teaspoons soft light brown sugar
1 teaspoon lemon juice

Steam the vegetables, except the cucumber, until just tender, removing the beansprouts after 5 minutes.

Put the coconut into a strainer set over a bowl, pour over the boiling water and leave to stand for 20 minutes, pressing the coconut to extract as much liquid as possible.

Arrange all the vegetables in bands on a large flat dish and garnish with hard-boiled eggs.

Fry separately in a little oil the chillies, then the garlic, then the blachan. Transfer them to a blender, add the peanut butter and coconut milk and process until smooth. Return the mixture to the pan, with the remaining ingredients and slowly bring to the boil, uncovered. Stir and pour over the salad.

COOK'S TIP

Blachan is an essential ingredient in south-east Asian cooking. It is made from prawns which have been salted, dried, pounded and allowed to ferment.

82 AEGEAN SALAD

Preparation time:
20 minutes

Serves 4

Calories:
187 per portion

YOU WILL NEED:
225 g/8 oz tomatoes, skinned
½ cucumber
1 green pepper
1 large mild onion
salt and pepper
3 tablespoons olive oil
1 tablespoon white wine vinegar
100 g/4 oz Greek Feta cheese
1 teaspoon dried oregano

Cut the tomatoes into quite thick slices. Peel the cucumber and cut it into thick slices. Halve the green pepper, discarding the stalk and seeds, and cut it into strips. Cut the onion in half, then slice each half thinly. Mix all these ingredients together in a salad bowl, adding salt and pepper to taste.

Stir in the oil and vinegar and mix well. Chop the Feta cheese roughly and scatter the pieces over the top of the salad. Sprinkle the dried oregano over all and mix lightly before serving.

COOK'S TIP

If fresh oregano is available, use this instead of dried. You will need about twice the amount given in this recipe.

83 TURKISH SALAD

Preparation time:
15 minutes

Serves 4

Calories:
340 per portion

YOU WILL NEED:
1 small white cabbage, finely shredded
200 g/7 oz large black olives, stoned
150 g/5 oz Feta cheese, crumbled
6 tablespoons olive oil
3 tablespoons lemon juice
½ teaspoon cumin seeds, crushed
pepper

Arrange the shredded cabbage in a large, shallow serving dish, then scatter the olives over and sprinkle the crumbled Feta on top.

Whisk together the oil, lemon juice and cumin seeds until well blended, then pour over the salad. Sprinkle with pepper.

COOK'S TIP

If Feta cheese is unobtainable, use a mixture of French goat's cheese and white Stilton. As the French cheese is less salty than Feta, you may need to add a little salt.

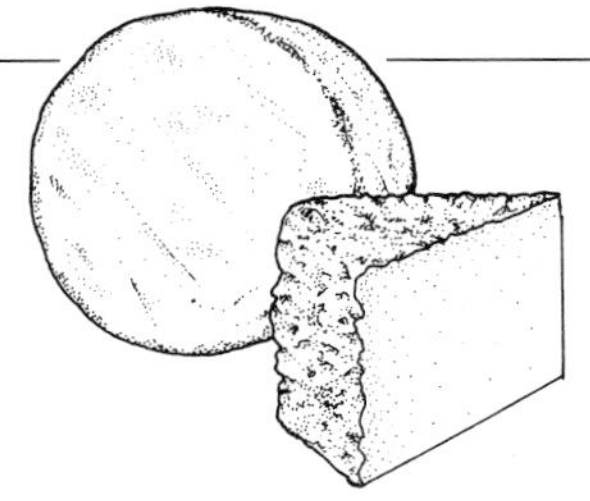

84 NEW YORK DELI SALAD

Preparation time:
20 minutes, plus standing

Serves 4

Calories:
286 per portion

YOU WILL NEED:
225 g/8 oz white cabbage, finely shredded
175 g/6 oz red cabbage, finely shredded
1 small onion, thinly sliced
50 g/2 oz walnuts, chopped
½ teaspoon caraway seeds, lightly crushed
1 teaspoon sultanas
1 teaspoon paprika, to sprinkle
FOR THE DRESSING
2 tablespoons cider vinegar or lemon juice
4 tablespoons olive oil
1 teaspoon clear honey
1 teaspoon French mustard
½ teaspoon salt
6 tablespoons soured cream

Combine the white and red cabbage, the onions, walnuts, caraway seeds and sultanas in a large salad bowl.

Mix all the dressing ingredients except the soured cream together in a jug, whisking with a fork until thoroughly blended. Pour over the salad and toss well. Leave to stand for 30 minutes.

Just before serving stir the soured cream briskly with a fork until smooth, then pour over the dressed salad and toss again. Sprinkle the salad with the paprika.

COOK'S TIP

You can replace the walnuts with drained and chopped, canned chestnuts. Coleslaw will keep well for a couple of days in the refrigerator.

85 MEXICAN SALAD

Preparation time:
15-20 minutes

Cooking time:
5-10 minutes

Serves 6

Calories:
233 per portion

YOU WILL NEED:
225 g/8 oz green beans, topped and tailed
50 g/2 oz blanched almonds, toasted and chopped
1 x 225 g/8 oz can red kidney beans, drained
50 g/2 oz cucumber, diced
1 x 225 g/8 oz can butter beans, drained
50 g/2 oz red pepper, halved, seeded and diced
FOR THE DRESSING
4½ tablespoons salad oil
1½ tablespoons wine vinegar
½ teaspoon annatto seeds
½ teaspoon sugar
½ teaspoon made mustard
1 tablespoon finely chopped fresh mint
salt and pepper

Cook the green beans in a saucepan of boiling salted water for 5-10 minutes until they are tender but still have some bite, then drain and place in a bowl. Mix the almonds with the green beans.

In a second bowl combine the kidney beans with the diced cucumber. Combine the butter beans with the diced red pepper in a third bowl.

Combine all the dressing ingredients, whisking with a fork to dissolve the sugar and mustard. Divide the dressing between the three bowls and stir well. Arrange the salads in three sections on a large serving dish.

COOK'S TIP

Annatto seeds, orangy-red in colour, are much used in Mexican and Caribbean cooking as a flavouring. If unobtainable, replace with saffron or turmeric.

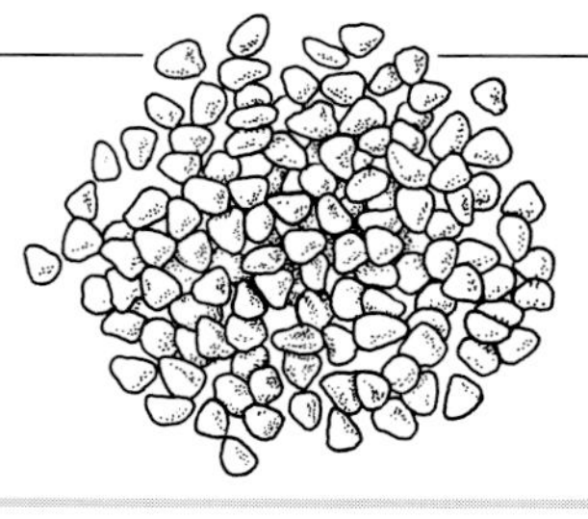

86 TABBOULEH

Preparation time:
15 minutes, plus soaking

Serves 4

Calories:
147 per portion

YOU WILL NEED:
75 g/3 oz bulgur wheat
1 teacup chopped parsley
3 tablespoons chopped fresh mint
4 spring onions, chopped
½ cucumber, finely diced
2 tablespoons olive oil
juice of 1 lemon
salt and pepper

Soak the bulgur wheat in cold water for 1 hour. Line a sieve with a piece of muslin and tip the wheat into it. Lift out the muslin, twist together and squeeze out as much moisture as possible from the wheat.

Place the wheat in a bowl and add the remaining ingredients, seasoning with salt and pepper to taste. Toss thoroughly, then transfer to a shallow dish to serve.

COOK'S TIP

Bulgur wheat, or burghul, is available in varying degrees of coarseness. Also called crushed wheat, it can be sprinkled on bread dough as a nutritious topping.

87 LEBANESE SALAD

Preparation time:
15 minutes, plus soaking

Serves 4

Calories:
247 per portion

YOU WILL NEED:
100 g/4 oz bulgur wheat (burghul)
2 bunches spring onions, chopped
225 g/8 oz tomatoes, skinned, chopped and drained
50 g/2 oz chopped parsley
4 tablespoons chopped fresh mint
4 tablespoons olive oil
3 tablespoons lemon juice
salt and pepper

Put the crushed wheat into a bowl and pour in fresh cold water to cover. Leave for 30 minutes, then drain and squeeze dry between your hands.

Put the crushed wheat into a bowl and add the spring onions, tomatoes, parsley and mint. Stir well to mix, then stir in the oil and lemon juice and season to taste with salt and pepper. Serve with cold meats, or with grilled kebabs, instead of rice.

COOK'S TIP

This very healthy salad, rich in Vitamin C, is a variation of tabbouleh. *Be sure to buy crushed wheat or burghul, as it is called in the Middle East: cracked wheat will not do.*

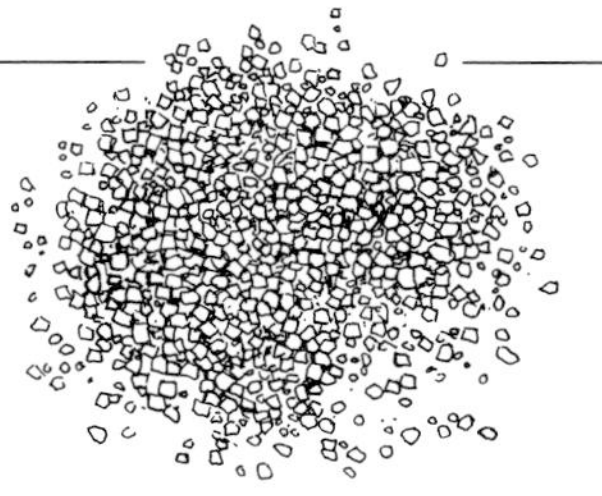

88 GREEK SALAD PITTA POCKETS

Preparation time:
20 minutes

Cooking time:
5-6 minutes

Serves 4

Calories:
235 per portion

YOU WILL NEED:
4 slices medium-sized pitta bread
FOR THE SALAD
100 g/4 oz cooked lamb, finely shredded
50 g/2 oz mushrooms, thinly sliced
1 small bunch spring onions, trimmed and chopped
2 lettuce leaves, shredded
2 tomatoes, skinned, seeded and chopped
4 black olives, stoned and sliced
2-3 tablespoons Yogurt dressing (see recipe 240)
salt and pepper
75 g/3 oz Cheddar cheese, grated

Carefully cut a slit across the top of each pitta bread but not through to the base. Gently open out the bread pockets each side of the slit.

Mix the lamb with the mushrooms, onions, lettuce, tomatoes, olives, yogurt dressing and salt and pepper to taste, blending well. Stuff the pitta pockets equally with this mixture and place on a grill rack. Sprinkle the cheese on top.

Place under a preheated moderate grill and cook for about 5-6 minutes until golden and bubbly. Serve at once whole or cut through into halves.

COOK'S TIP

Slices of pitta bread can also be filled with a West Indian mixture of ingredients: 100 g/4 oz cooked diced chicken mixed with 50 g/2 oz finely chopped pineapple, 50 g/2 oz chopped green pepper, 1 small sliced banana, 25 g/1 oz toasted almonds, 2-3 tablespoons mayonnaise and salt and pepper to taste. Top with the cheese and grill.

MAINLY VEGETABLES

Vegetables, in all their wonderful variety of texture, flavour, colour and shape, form the basis for the salads here. Follow the recipes exactly, or use them as a jumping-off point for creating your own unique mixtures of vegetables and flavourings. Try different dressings, too, choosing from the collection in the last chapter.

89 PASTA, PEA AND ARTICHOKE SALAD

Preparation time:
15 minutes

Cooking time:
about 10 minutes

Serves 4

Calories:
360 per portion

YOU WILL NEED:
225 g/8 oz coloured pasta bows or shells
1 x 425 g/15 oz can artichoke hearts, drained and sliced
425 g/15 oz petit pois, defrosted if frozen
1 canned sweet pimiento, drained and diced
½ teaspoon freshly grated nutmeg
salt and pepper
FOR THE DRESSING
1 tablespoon white vermouth
1 tablespoon lemon juice
3 tablespoons olive oil
4 tablespoons soured cream

Cook the pasta in boiling salted water for about 10 minutes or according to packet instructions until *al dente*. Drain.

Turn the pasta into a large salad bowl and add the artichoke hearts, peas and pimiento. Sprinkle with the nutmeg, season with salt and pepper and turn gently with two forks, making sure the pasta does not break up.

Combine all the dressing ingredients in a jug, whisking with a fork until smooth, then pour over the salad and fork through lightly to coat all the ingredients with dressing. Serve the salad at room temperature.

COOK'S TIP

Coloured pastas get their colour from natural vegetable colours; spinach dyes pasta green and tomatoes dye it red.

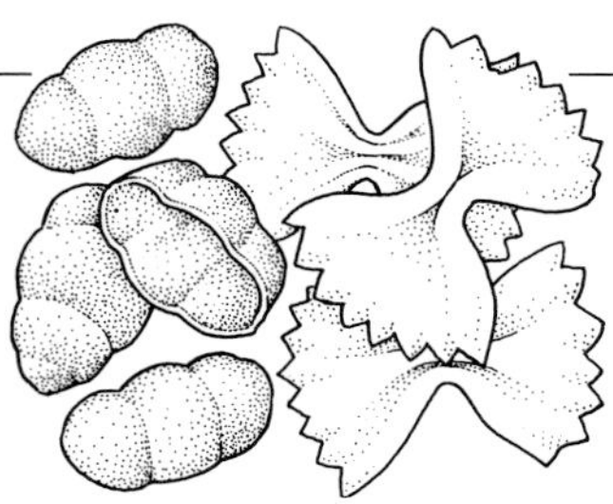

90 MUSHROOM AND BEANSPROUT SALAD

Preparation time:
10 minutes

Serves 4

Calories:
11 per portion

YOU WILL NEED:
100 g/4 oz button mushrooms, finely sliced
175 g/6 oz beansprouts
FOR THE DRESSING
3 tablespoons olive oil
4 tablespoons fresh orange juice
1 tablespoon finely grated lemon rind
salt and pepper

First make the dressing: put the dressing ingredients in a small bowl and whisk together thoroughly.

Put the mushroom slices and beansprouts in a bowl, pour over the dressing and toss well together.

COOK'S TIP

Serve this delicious, crunchy salad with mild-flavoured pork dishes and with meat and poultry dishes served with rice.

91 MUSHROOM SALAD

Preparation time:
10 minutes

Serves 4

Calories:
132 per portion

YOU WILL NEED:
225 g/8 oz very fresh button mushrooms
salt and pepper
2 tablespoons finely chopped onion
1 garlic clove
4 tablespoons olive oil
1 tablespoon white wine vinegar
½ tablespoon lemon juice
2 tablespoons chopped chervil
2 tablespoons chopped chives

Wipe the mushrooms with a damp cloth; remove the stalks and cut the caps into thin slices. Put them in a serving bowl and add lots of coarse salt and black pepper. Stir in the chopped onion and crushed garlic. Stir in the oil and vinegar, then the lemon juice and the chopped herbs.

COOK'S TIP

Serve this salad soon after it is made, or the mushrooms will dry up and need more oil added.

92 MUSHROOM CABBAGE SLAW

Preparation time:
15 minutes, plus chilling

Serves 4

Calories:
108 per portion

YOU WILL NEED:
225 g/8 oz mushrooms (see Cook's Tip)
225 g/8 oz white cabbage
50 g/2 oz sultanas
300 ml/½ pint natural yogurt
2 tablespoons lemon juice
2 tablespoons Dijon mustard
salt and pepper
2 tablespoons chopped fresh chives

Slice the mushrooms thinly and shred the cabbage.

Mix the mushrooms, cabbage and sultanas together in a bowl.

Stir in the yogurt, lemon juice, mustard, salt and pepper together. Pour over the mushroom mixture and mix well.

Cover the bowl and chill overnight.

Stir before serving then sprinkle with the chives.

COOK'S TIP

Use button or small cap mushrooms in this recipe, removing the stalks and wiping them clean before slicing them.

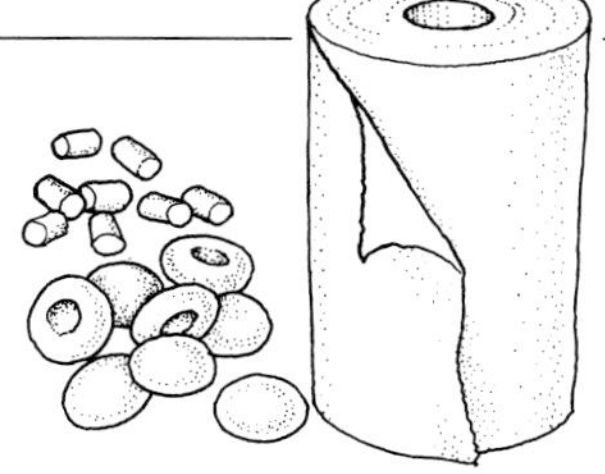

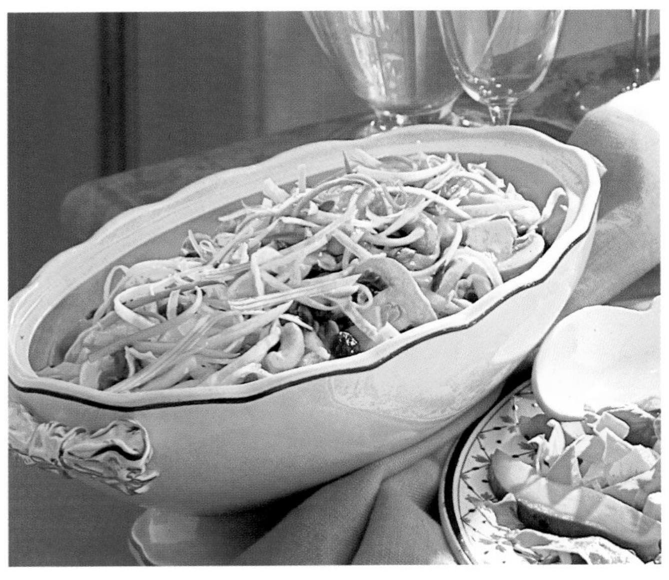

93 SWEET CABBAGE SALAD

Preparation time:
20 minutes, plus marinating

Serves 4

Calories:
156 per portion

YOU WILL NEED:
350 g/12 oz white cabbage, shredded
100 g/4 oz button mushrooms, sliced
6 tablespoons sultanas
4 tablespoons pumpkin seeds
4 tablespoons cashew nuts
FOR THE DRESSING
2 tablespoons clear honey
1 tablespoon lemon juice
1 teaspoon lemon rind
1 teaspoon cider vinegar
salt and pepper
3 tablespoons natural yogurt
spring onions, to garnish

Mix the dressing ingredients together.

Toss together the cabbage, mushrooms and sultanas. Pour on the dressing, toss well and leave at room temperature for about 30 minutes.

Stir in the pumpkin seeds and nuts.

Garnish with spring onions before serving.

COOK'S TIP

This is another salad that accompanies grilled or cold poultry and meats well. It is also a good salad for serving on mixed buffet tables, its pale colour contrasting well with green and mixed salads.

94 CASHEW COLESLAW

Preparation time:
10 minutes

Serves 6-8

Calories:
304-228 per portion

YOU WILL NEED:
225 g/8 oz firm white cabbage, shredded
3 celery sticks, sliced
3 red-skinned dessert apples, cored and thinly sliced
4 spring onions, sliced
50 g/2 oz cashew nuts, toasted
2 tablespoons chopped parsley
150 ml/¼ pint mayonnaise
2 tablespoons natural yogurt

Place the cabbage, celery, apples, spring onions, cashews and parsley in a mixing bowl.

Mix the mayonnaise and yogurt together, then pour over the salad and toss thoroughly. Transfer to a salad bowl to serve.

COOK'S TIP

A commercially-prepared mayonnaise would go well in this salad. The cashew nuts could be replaced by walnuts, if liked.

95 GREEN AND WHITE VEGETABLE SALAD

Preparation time:
15 minutes

Serves 4

Calories:
283 per portion

YOU WILL NEED:
50 g/2 oz frozen green peas, thawed
100 g/4 oz white cabbage, thinly sliced
2 celery sticks, chopped
1 small green pepper, cored, seeded and chopped
½ onion or ½ leek, thinly sliced
100 g/4 oz Brussels sprouts, quartered
100 g/4 oz bean sprouts
4 tablespoons French dressing (see recipe 233)

Mix all the vegetables together in a salad bowl. Pour over the dressing and toss well. Serve immediately.

COOK'S TIP

A simple vegetable slicer or a food processor fitted with a slicing blade will considerably cut down the preparation time and give finely, evenly sliced vegetables.

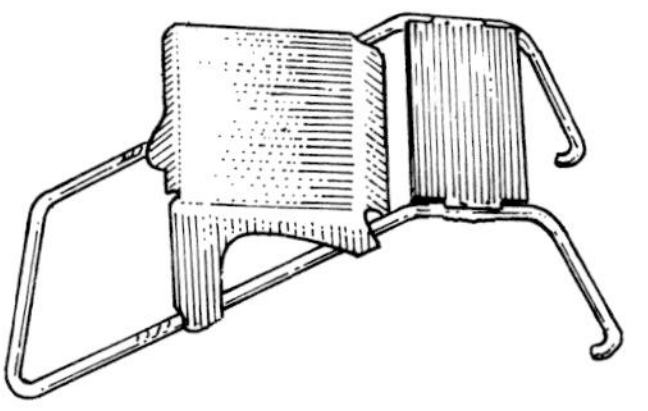

96 CABBAGE SALAD WITH PEANUT DRESSING

Preparation time:
15 minutes

Serves 4

Calories:
191 per portion

YOU WILL NEED:
1 small white cabbage, finely sliced
100 g/4 oz salted peanuts, chopped
2 red peppers, cored, seeded and finely chopped
1 teaspoon anchovy essence (see Cook's Tip)
1 tablespoon soy sauce
2 tablespoons lemon juice
1 teaspoon cayenne pepper
½ teaspoon salt
1 teaspoon soft brown sugar

Put the cabbage in a salad bowl. Combine the remaining ingredients to form a crunchy sauce. Spoon over the cabbage and serve immediately.

COOK'S TIP

Anchovy essence is a commercially-made flavouring, based on the pounded flesh of anchovies. If it is not available, one or two chopped anchovy fillets could be added to this salad instead.

97 RED CABBAGE WITH SOURED CREAM DRESSING

Preparation time:
5 minutes, plus standing

Serves 4

Calories:
123 per portion

YOU WILL NEED:
1 small red cabbage, about 350 g/12 oz, shredded
1 small onion, finely sliced
1 large tart dessert apple, peeled, cored and sliced
1 teaspoon cumin seeds, crushed to a powder
1 tablespoon poppy seeds
FOR THE DRESSING
150 ml/5 fl oz soured cream
2 teaspoons Dijon mustard
1 tablespoon wine vinegar or lemon juice
2 teaspoons sugar
salt

Put the cabbage, onion and apple in a large salad bowl and fork through to mix. Sprinkle with the cumin and poppy seeds.

Combine all the dressing ingredients and whisk with a fork to blend thoroughly. Pour over the salad and toss with 2 salad spoons to distribute evenly.

COOK'S TIP

All kinds of onions tend to become bitter if the cut flesh is exposed to the air too long before use, so ensure the salad is well covered with its dressing as soon as possible after the vegetables have been prepared.

98 RED, WHITE AND YELLOW SALAD

Preparation time:
20 minutes

Serves 6

Calories:
159 per portion

YOU WILL NEED:
½ small or ¼ medium red cabbage, very finely shredded
¼ small white cabbage, very finely shredded
3 yellow peppers, seeded and finely chopped
120 ml/4 fl oz mayonnaise
4 tablespoons natural yogurt
¼ teaspoon ground caraway
¼ teaspoon dill seeds, crushed
salt and pepper

Combine the shredded cabbages and yellow peppers in a large salad bowl.

Mix together the mayonnaise, yogurt, ground caraway and dill seeds, stirring thoroughly, then pour over the salad. Toss to coat all the vegetables with some of the dressing, then season generously with salt and freshly ground black pepper.

COOK'S TIP

Caraway has a special affinity with cabbage, so is the ideal spice to use in this salad. Its characteristic pungent flavour will spread through the salad in powder form well.

99 CHINESE CABBAGE AND WATERCRESS SALAD

Preparation time:
10 minutes

Serves 6

Calories:
93 per portion

YOU WILL NEED:
1 small Chinese cabbage, shredded
1 bunch of watercress
4 oranges, segmented
5 tablespoons Mint and honey dressing (see recipe 208)

Put the cabbage, watercress and orange segments in a salad bowl. Pour in the dressing and toss well. Serve immediately.

100 CABBAGE SALAD WITH DILL

Preparation time:
15 minutes

Serves 4

Calories:
183 per portion

YOU WILL NEED:
1/4 Chinese cabbage or 1/4 hard white cabbage
1/2 cucumber
1/2 bunch spring onions
salt and pepper
3 tablespoons sunflower seed oil
1 tablespoon white wine vinegar
4 hard-boiled eggs
2 tablespoons chopped dill

Wash and drain the cabbage and cut it across in thin strips. Pile it into a salad bowl. Peel the cucumber and cut it in half lengthwise, then in semi-circular slices. Slice the spring onions, using the white bulbs and the best of the green leaves.

Mix all together and add salt and pepper to taste. Stir in the oil and vinegar and mix thoroughly. Shell the eggs, cut in half lengthwise then in semi-circular slices. Mix lightly into the salad, adding the chopped dill at the same time.

COOK'S TIP

Use the variety of Chinese cabbage called Pe-tsai *in this recipe as its pale colour contrasts well with the dark green of the peppery-flavoured watercress.*

COOK'S TIP

Dill, an aromatic, sweetly flavoured herb, has the useful property of having a calming effect on the stomach, so is excellent with raw vegetables that may be indigestible.

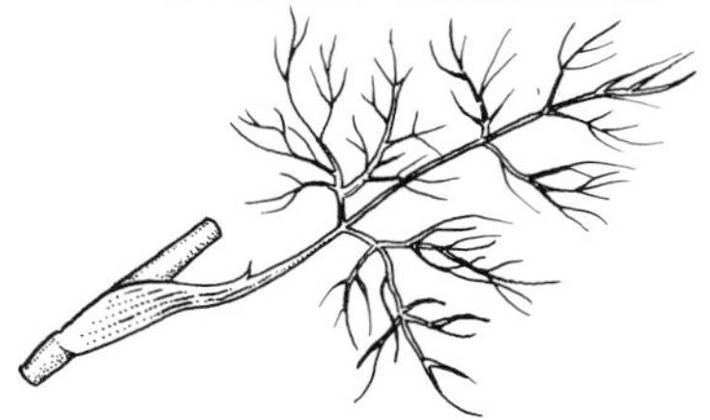

101 TOMATOES WITH HORSERADISH AND DILL

Preparation time:
10-12 minutes

Cooking time:
1 minute

Serves 4

Calories:
365 per portion

YOU WILL NEED:
450 g/1 lb small tomatoes, skinned
150 ml/¼ pint mayonnaise
65 ml/2½ fl oz soured cream
65 ml/2½ fl oz natural yogurt
2 teaspoons lemon juice
4 tablespoons grated horseradish
1½ tablespoons chopped fresh dill
1 sprig dill, to garnish

Pile the tomatoes in a pyramid on a flat dish. In a bowl combine the mayonnaise with the soured cream and yogurt, then stir in the lemon juice, horseradish and dill.

Spoon the horseradish sauce over the tomatoes just before serving and garnish with the dill sprig.

COOK'S TIP

Try using tiny cherry tomatoes in this salad. They would not need to be skinned.

102 TOMATO AND BASIL SALAD

Preparation time:
10 minutes, plus standing

Serves 4

Calories:
107 per portion

YOU WILL NEED:
750 g/1½ lb large ripe tomatoes, sliced
freshly ground black pepper
½ teaspoon sugar
3 tablespoons olive oil
1 tablespoon white wine vinegar
2 tablespoons fresh basil, cut into thin strips
1 sprig basil, to garnish

Arrange the tomato slices neatly overlapping on a large flat serving dish. Season with plenty of pepper and sprinkle over the sugar.

Combine the oil and vinegar and spoon evenly over the tomatoes. Leave to stand for 1 hour. Just before serving, scatter the basil over the tomatoes. Serve garnished with a basil sprig.

COOK'S TIP

Basil and tomatoes make a perfect first-course salad. For a summer lunch dish, add 175 g/6 oz thinly sliced Mozzarella cheese.

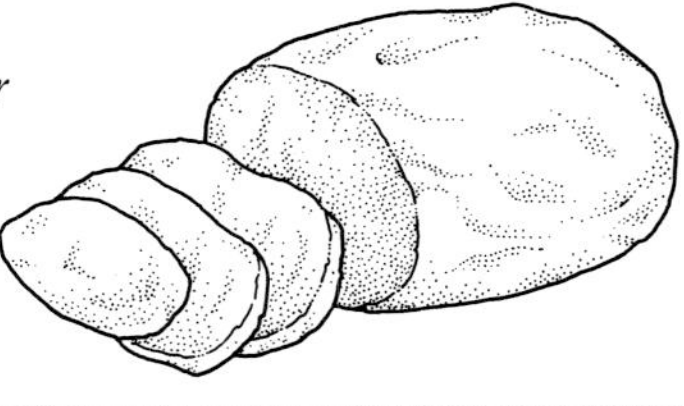

103 CRUNCHY SALAD

Preparation time:
5 minutes

Cooking time:
1 minute

Serves 4

Calories:
268 per portion

YOU WILL NEED:
225 g/8 oz green pepper, cored, seeded and chopped
225 g/8 oz fennel, finely chopped
225 g/8 oz celery, roughly chopped
1 cucumber, peeled and diced
100 g/4 oz spring onions, chopped
1-2 teaspoons chopped fresh tarragon
4-5 tablespoons Lemon vinaigrette (see recipe 227)

Blanch the green pepper in boiling water for 1 minute. Drain.

Mix the pepper, fennel, celery, cucumber and spring onions together in a salad bowl and sprinkle with the tarragon. Spoon the Lemon vinaigrette over the salad and mix well together.

COOK'S TIP

For a more pronounced herb flavour in this salad, replace the tarragon and Lemon vinaigrette with Vinaigrette with mixed herbs (see recipe 237).

104 GRILLED PEPPER SALAD

Preparation time:
20 minutes, plus cooling

Cooking time:
15-20 minutes

Serves 4

Calories:
136 per portion

YOU WILL NEED:
2 green peppers
1 red pepper
1 yellow pepper (or an extra red pepper)
2 garlic cloves, finely chopped
2 small onions, thinly sliced into rings
2 tablespoons chopped parsley
2 tablespoons black olives
1 x 40 g/1½ oz can anchovy fillets, drained
FOR THE DRESSING
3 tablespoons olive oil
2 teaspoons lemon juice
pepper

Place the peppers under a preheated moderately high grill for about 15-20 minutes, turning them frequently, until their skins blacken. Cover with a damp cloth and leave them to cool. Peel.

Core and seed the peppers and cut them into thick slices. Toss the peppers with the chopped garlic and the onion rings.

Bring the oil and lemon juice just to boiling point. Pour over the peppers and mix well. Leave to cool. Season with pepper. Stir the parsley and olives into the salad. Turn into a serving dish and garnish with the anchovy fillets.

COOK'S TIP

Major supermarkets usually have a variety of different coloured peppers. Be careful to choose ones that will fit under the grill.

105 HOT CUCUMBER SALAD

Preparation time:
15 minutes

Cooking time:
5-10 minutes

Serves 4

Calories:
18 per portion, plus dressing

YOU WILL NEED:
2-3 tablespoons French dressing (recipe 233)
1 small cucumber, thinly sliced but not peeled
1 garlic clove, finely chopped
1 large Cos lettuce heart, washed and shredded
1 tablespoon fresh finely chopped dill
2 tablespoons lemon juice
salt and pepper
1 tablespoon finely chopped parsley, to garnish

Put the dressing in a pan on a moderate heat and cook the cucumber and garlic in it until the cucumber is just beginning to soften. Quickly stir in the lettuce, dill and lemon juice. Season to taste and serve immediately, garnished with the chopped parsley.

COOK'S TIP

This warm, slightly tart salad is an ideal one to serve with grilled steak or lamb chops.

106 GREEN SALAD WITH A HERB SAUCE

Preparation time:
10 minutes

Serves 4

Calories:
141 per portion

YOU WILL NEED:
1 round lettuce
1 batavia (see Cook's Tip)
100 g/4 oz corn salad (mâche)
FOR THE HERB SAUCE
2 hard-boiled eggs
2 tablespoons thick cream
2 tablespoons olive oil
2 teaspoons white wine vinegar
salt and pepper
1 tablespoon chopped chives
1 tablespoon chopped dill
1 tablespoon chopped tarragon

Break the lettuce leaves in pieces and pile in a salad bowl. Using only the pale green inner leaves of the batavia, scatter them over the lettuce and put the corn salad on top.

Separate the whites and yolks of the hard-boiled eggs.

Chop the egg whites and scatter over the green salad. Mash the egg yolks to a paste with the cream, and stir in the oil very gradually. Then add the vinegar slowly and stir until blended. Add salt and pepper to taste, and stir in the herbs. Pour the herb sauce over the greens and mix well.

COOK'S TIP

Batavia, also called escarole, is a type of endive. Though slightly less curly-leaved than the more familiar curly endive, it has a similar slightly bitter taste.

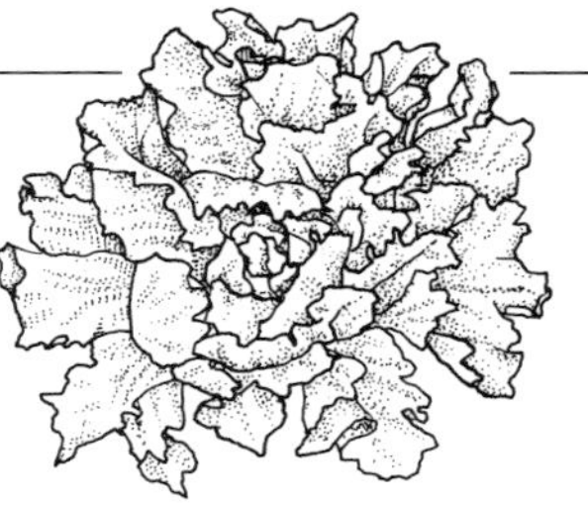

107 CUCUMBER AND FENNEL SALAD

Preparation time:
15 minutes

Serves 4

Calories:
22 per portion, plus dressing

YOU WILL NEED:
1 large cucumber
75 g/3 oz fennel
2 tablespoons finely chopped parsley
1 small onion, finely sliced
1 box mustard and cress
3-4 tablespoons French dressing (see recipe 233)

Wash and finely slice the unpeeled cucumber and place it in a salad bowl. Wash and grate the fennel and add to the cucumber with all the remaining ingredients. Toss lightly and serve.

COOK'S TIP

For a less pungent onion flavour in this salad, use 1 or 2 shallots or half a red onion instead of the standard white onion.

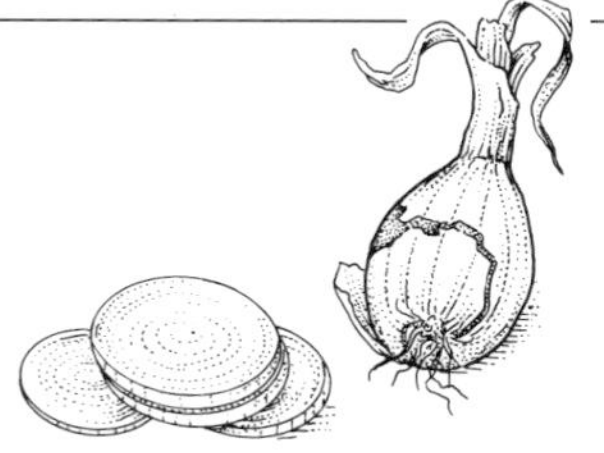

108 CHINESE CUCUMBER AND RADISH SALAD

Preparation time:
25 minutes, plus salting

Serves 4

Calories:
72 per portion

YOU WILL NEED:
1 medium cucumber, peeled, halved lengthways, seeded and thinly sliced
2 teaspoons salt
1 mooli (Japanese radish), peeled, halved lengthways and thinly sliced
2 large spring onions, thinly sliced
FOR THE DRESSING
2 tablespoons light soy sauce
1 tablespoon vegetable oil
1 teaspoon wine vinegar
1 teaspoon sesame oil
salt
½ teaspoon caster sugar

Put the cucumber in a colander, sprinkle with salt, set over a plate and leave for 20 minutes, to extract the juices. Rinse the cucumber under cold running water and pat dry with absorbent paper.

Put the cucumber in a salad bowl with the mooli and spring onions.

Thoroughly combine all the dressing ingredients in a jug, then pour over the salad and toss lightly with a fork to coat all the vegetables.

Serve the salad at once.

COOK'S TIP

This salad is a good one to serve with cold meats or with grilled pork chops.

109 CAULIFLOWER AND WATERCRESS SALAD

Preparation time:
10 minutes, plus cooling

Cooking time:
3 minutes

Serves 4

Calories:
375 per portion

YOU WILL NEED:
1 small cauliflower, broken into florets
salt
1 bunch watercress
4 spring onions, chopped
5 tablespoons French dressing (see recipe 233)
1 tablespoon sesame seeds, roasted (see Cook's Tip)

Cook the cauliflower in boiling salted water for 3 minutes; drain and cool. Add the watercress, spring onions and dressing and toss thoroughly.

Transfer to a salad bowl and sprinkle with the sesame seeds. Serve the salad immediately.

COOK'S TIP

To roast sesame seeds, place the seeds in a single layer on a baking sheet. Roast in a moderate oven (180 C/350 F/ Gas 4) for about 15 minutes, until golden brown. To toast the seeds, shake them in a heavy-based pan over a moderate heat for about a minute or put them under a moderate grill, shaking to turn them.

110 CAULIFLOWER AND CRESS SALAD

Preparation time:
5 minutes, plus cooling

Cooking time:
1 minute

Serves 4

Calories:
332 per portion

YOU WILL NEED:
450 g/1 lb cauliflower, broken into florets
salt
1 carton mustard and cress, trimmed
25 g/1 oz pumpkin seeds
4 tablespoons French dressing (see recipe 233)

Cook the cauliflower in boiling salted water for 1 minute; drain and leave to cool completely. Place in a bowl with the remaining ingredients and toss thoroughly. Transfer to a shallow dish and serve.

COOK'S TIP

The easiest way to trim mustard and cress is simply to cut it off the growing medium in the carton with scissors.

111 DOMINO SALAD

Preparation time:
20 minutes

Cooking time:
10 minutes

Serves 4

Calories:
176 per portion

YOU WILL NEED:
1 small cauliflower, divided into florets
salt
100 g/4 oz dried chick peas, soaked overnight and cooked
4 tablespoons black olives
1 bunch watercress
chicory leaves
FOR THE DRESSING
3 tablespoons olive oil
1 tablespoon cider vinegar
1 hard-boiled egg, roughly chopped
1 tablespoon soured cream
salt and pepper

Cook the cauliflower in boiling, salted water for about 8 minutes, until it is barely tender. Drain, plunge into cold water and drain again. Leave to cool.

Mix the dressing in a blender to emulsify the ingredients. Check the seasoning.

Mix the cauliflower, chick peas, olives and watercress. Pour on the dressing and toss well. Line a dish with the chicory leaves and arrange the salad on top.

COOK'S TIP

If soured cream is not available, use ordinary thick cream and add ½ teaspoon of lemon juice to the dressing.

112 COURGETTES AND YOGURT

Preparation time:
10 minutes, plus draining

Serves 4

Calories:
73 per portion

YOU WILL NEED:
8 small courgettes, peeled
lemon juice
300 ml/½ pint natural yogurt
salt and pepper

Thinly slice or grate the courgettes.

Mix enough lemon juice into the yogurt to make a fluid consistency. Add salt and pepper to taste.

Mix the courgettes and yogurt together. Serve this salad at a curry meal, or with plainly grilled white fish.

COOK'S TIP

Use a medium cucumber instead of the courgettes. Leave the skin on, if liked, and drain the sliced or grated cucumber well in a colander or sieve.

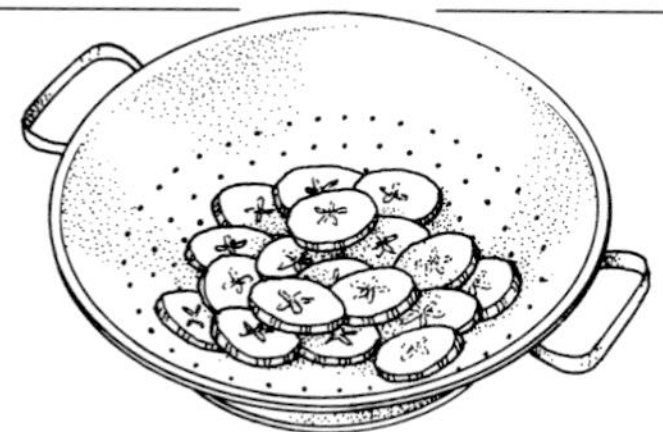

113 HOT POTATO SALAD

Preparation time:
10 minutes, plus cooling

Cooking time:
about 12 minutes

Serves 4

Calories:
245 per portion

YOU WILL NEED:
675 g/1½ lb new or waxy potatoes
2 tablespoons finely chopped onion
3 tablespoons olive oil
1 tablespoon white wine vinegar
salt and pepper
4 tablespoons chopped chives

Wash the potatoes and cook them in their skins in boiling salted water. Peel them as soon as they are cool enough to handle. Cut into quarters or thick slices, put into a bowl and stir in the chopped onion. Pour over the oil and vinegar, and mix gently, trying not to break the potatoes. Add salt and pepper to taste. Stir in 3 tablespoons of the chives.

Turn the salad into a serving dish and scatter the remaining chives over the top.

COOK'S TIP

Spring onion tops, finely chopped, make a good substitute for the chives in this recipe.

114 POTATO SALAD

Preparation time:
10 minutes

Cooking time:
about 12 minutes

Serves 6

Calories:
537 per portion

YOU WILL NEED:
675 g/1½ lb new or waxy potatoes
4 tablespoons thin cream
150 ml/¼ pint Mayonnaise (see recipe 219)
salt and pepper
3 tablespoons chopped chervil

Wash the potatoes and cook them in their skins in boiling salted water. As soon as they are cool enough to handle, skin them, slice thickly and put into a bowl.

Add the cream to the mayonnaise to thin it, and stir into the potatoes while they are still warm. Add salt and pepper to taste, and stir in the chopped chervil. Serve the potato salad soon after making it.

COOK'S TIP

Chervil gives a refreshingly spicy flavour to this salad. Since it grows easily in gardens or window boxes it can be used with a generous hand.

115 CREAMED POTATO SALAD IN SHELLS

Preparation time:
10 minutes, plus cooling

Cooking time:
25 minutes

Serves 6

Calories:
172 per portion

YOU WILL NEED:
750 g/1 ¾ lb potatoes, cut into even-sized pieces
2 medium onions, finely chopped
6 tablespoons finely chopped fresh parsley
2 tablespoons olive oil
100 ml/3 ½ fl oz cider vinegar
salt and pepper
6 scallop shells, to serve

Bring a large pan of salted water to the boil, add the potatoes and cook for 20-25 minutes until very soft.

Drain the potatoes then put them into a bowl. Mash them coarsely, then add the onions, parsley, oil, vinegar, a little salt and a generous amount of freshly ground black pepper. Mash thoroughly until completely smooth, then taste. If the potatoes are floury, they may need another 1-2 tablespoons oil. They should taste well seasoned, but avoid adding too much, especially salt.

Divide the creamed potato among the shells and leave, covered, in a cool place for 2 hours. They should be served cold but not chilled. Fluff up the tops with a fork just before serving.

COOK'S TIP

Scallop shells may be bought from fishmongers. Sterilize them by boiling in water for 5 minutes, then peel away any loose bits and leave the shells to dry. Lightly oil them inside and out just before using.

116 VEGETABLE SALAD WITH HERB SAUCE

Preparation time:
15 minutes, plus cooling

Cooking time:
about 15 minutes

Serves 4

Calories:
345 per portion

YOU WILL NEED:
175 g/6 oz new potatoes, washed
2 tablespoons olive oil
175 g/6 oz courgettes
175 g/6 oz string beans
1 bunch spring onions
1 lettuce
1 x recipe Herb sauce (see recipe 106)

Boil the potatoes in their skins. Skin while hot and cut into slices. Pour over 1 tablespoon olive oil and leave to cool. Slice the courgettes. Drop them into a saucepan containing a little boiling salted water, cover the pan and cook for 10 minutes. Drain and sprinkle with ½ tablespoon olive oil. Cut the beans into 2.5 cm/1 in pieces. Boil them until just tender, drain and sprinkle with ½ tablespoon olive oil. Trim the spring onions. Break the lettuce leaves into pieces and put them in a salad bowl. Cover with the potatoes, courgettes, beans and spring onions. Pour the Herb sauce over the salad and mix well.

COOK'S TIP

Use only fresh herbs in this sauce. Other herbs which could be used in place of those mentioned here include parsley, apple mint and fennel tops.

117 ROMAN SALAD

Preparation time:
15 minutes

Cooking time:
about 15 minutes

Serves 4

Calories:
252 per portion

YOU WILL NEED:
225 g/8 oz shelled broad beans
salt
225 g/8 oz young spinach leaves, finely shredded
100 g/4 oz button mushrooms, thinly sliced
3 large firm tomatoes, skinned, seeded and chopped
a few sprigs of fennel leaves, or parsley
FOR THE DRESSING
3 tablespoons olive oil
1 tablespoon cider vinegar
pepper
1 tablespoon clear honey
½ teaspoon mustard powder
50 g/2 oz Mozzarella cheese, cubed

Cook the beans in boiling, salted water until they are just tender. Drain, plunge at once into cold water and drain again. Leave to cool. Mix the dressing.

Toss together the beans, spinach, mushrooms and tomatoes. Just before serving, pour on the dressing and toss well. Garnish with the fennel leaves or other herb sprigs.

COOK'S TIP

Serve this salad as soon as possible after pouring on the dressing as the young spinach will lose its crispness if left in the dressing too long.

118 BROAD BEAN SALAD

Preparation time:
10 minutes

Serves 4

Calories:
245 per portion

YOU WILL NEED:
225 g/8 oz young fresh spinach, trimmed
450 g/1 lb cooked shelled broad beans
100 g/4 oz cooked peas
4 tomatoes, sliced
6-8 tablespoons Lemon vinaigrette (see recipe 227)

Shred the spinach leaves. Arrange in a serving dish.

Mix the beans and peas together and place in the centre of the spinach.

Arrange the tomato slices around the beans. Drizzle the Lemon vinaigrette over the salad.

COOK'S TIP

If fresh broad beans are out of season, use frozen beans, which retain a good flavour. Do not remove the skins round the beans – they are an excellent source of fibre.

119 BROAD BEAN MAYONNAISE

Preparation time:
10 minutes

Cooking time:
10 minutes

Serves 6

Calories:
148 per portion

YOU WILL NEED:
450 g/1 lb shelled broad beans
salt
juice of ½ lemon
1 teaspoon oil
3 tablespoons natural yogurt
4 tablespoons Mayonnaise (see recipe 219)
1 tablespoon chopped mixed herbs (parsley, thyme and chives)

Cook the beans in boiling salted water for 10 minutes, then drain and place in a bowl. Mix with the lemon juice and oil and leave to cool.

Mix together the yogurt, mayonnaise and most of the herbs. Pour over the beans and mix well. Transfer to a salad bowl and sprinkle with the remaining herbs before serving.

COOK'S TIP

Other fresh herbs which go well in this salad include chervil, savory and salad burnet.

120 SPROUTED BEAN SALAD

Preparation time:
25 minutes, plus soaking

Serves 4

Calories:
145 per portion

YOU WILL NEED:
225 g/8 oz sprouted beans or peas, such as alfalfa, mung or chick peas
4 spring onions, thinly sliced
½ small cucumber, diced
8 large radishes, thinly sliced
4 tablespoons cashew nuts
2 hard-boiled eggs, quartered
FOR THE DRESSING
150 ml/¼ pint natural yogurt
1 teaspoon clear honey
2 teaspoons soy sauce
1 teaspoon red wine vinegar
1 tablespoon dry sherry
salt and pepper
4 spring onions tassels, to garnish

Mix the dressing and pour it into 4 individual serving bowls.

Toss together the sprouted beans, spring onions, cucumber, radish slices and nuts. Divide the salad between the bowls.

Arrange the egg wedges on top of the salad. Garnish each dish with a spring onion frill.

COOK'S TIP

To 'sprout' beans or peas, select clean whole seeds and soak in cold water overnight. Drain and place in a large glass jar. Cover the jar with muslin, securing with a rubber band. Two or three times a day, pour cold water through the muslin, then drain it off. The seeds should sprout in 4-5 days.

121 CARROT AND ORANGE SALAD

Preparation time:
15 minutes

Serves 4

Calories:
152 per portion, plus dressing

YOU WILL NEED:
2 large carrots, scraped
4 oranges
1 head of chicory
lettuce leaves
Orange vinaigrette (see Cook's Tip, recipe 227), to serve

Grate the carrots coarsely. Peel and discard the skin and pith from the oranges, then slice the flesh thinly into rounds, removing all the pips.

Slice the chicory thinly.

Arrange the lettuce on a shallow serving dish and attractively arrange the grated carrot and orange and chicory slices on top. Serve the Orange vinaigrette separately.

COOK'S TIP

Green olives, echoing the flavour of the olive oil in the vinaigrette, make an interesting additional ingredient in this salad; allow 50-75 g/2-3 oz.

122 CARROT AND RAISIN SALAD

Preparation time:
10 minutes, plus standing

Serves 4

Calories:
75 per portion

YOU WILL NEED:
450 g/1 lb carrots, grated
75 g/ 3 oz raisins
2 tablespoons soy sauce
chopped parsley, to garnish

Put the carrot and raisins in a serving dish and mix them well together.

Sprinkle over the soy sauce and toss well. Allow the salad to stand for 5-10 minutes, for the flavours to blend. Garnish with chopped parsley before serving.

COOK'S TIP

A good variation on this simple salad is to replace half the carrot with coarsely grated white cabbage.

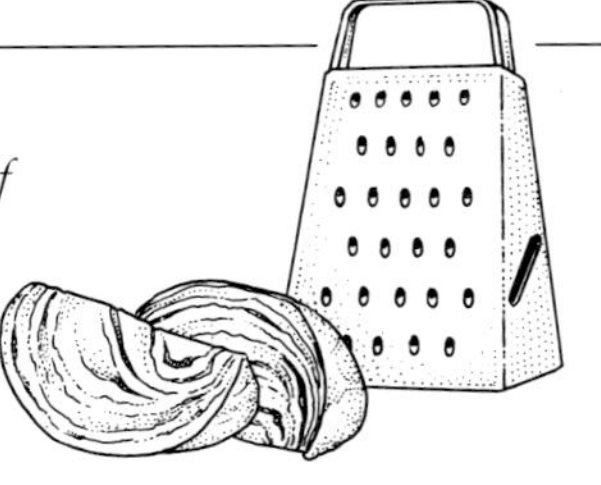

123 VEGETABLE STRAWS

Preparation time:
30 minutes

Cooking time:
10 minutes

Serves 4

Calories:
223 per portion

YOU WILL NEED:
350 g/12 oz French beans
350 g/12 oz carrots, cut in matchstick strips about 9 cm/3½ inches long
1 small red pepper, cored, seeded and sliced into rings
1 small green pepper, cored, seeded and sliced into rings
a few Chinese lettuce leaves, shredded
½ bunch watercress
4 tablespoons toasted almonds
FOR THE DRESSING
4 tablespoons sunflower oil
1 tablespoon red wine vinegar
2 teaspoons orange juice
1 teaspoon orange rind
1 garlic clove, crushed
½ teaspoon mustard powder
1 tablespoon finely snipped chives

Cook the beans and carrots separately in boiling, salted water until just tender. Drain, plunge them into cold water and drain again. Blanch the pepper rings in boiling salted water for 1 minute, then drain. Mix the dressing and season it to taste.

Toss together the Chinese leaves, watercress and almonds and pile on a flat serving dish.

Gather up the beans and carrots into bundles of 5 or 6 and push each through a pepper ring of the alternative colour.

Arrange alternate bunches of beans and carrots around the dish. Pour the dressing over.

COOK'S TIP

To add a third colour – cream – to the vegetable straws, try matchsticks of fresh celery, lightly cooked, or of canned palm hearts.

124 HI-FI SALAD WITH PEANUT SAUCE

Preparation time:
30 minutes

Cooking time:
15 minutes

Serves 6

Calories:
246 per portion

YOU WILL NEED:
225 g/8 oz young French beans
2 leeks, thinly sliced
450 g/1 lb tomatoes, cut into wedges
4 celery sticks, sliced
1 tablespoon sunflower oil
1 teaspoon lemon juice
freshly ground black pepper
FOR THE SAUCE
100 g/4 oz raw peanuts
about 4 tablespoons oil
1 tablespoon red wine vinegar
1 medium onion, chopped
1 garlic clove, halved
½ teaspoon chilli powder (or to taste)
sugar

Cook the beans in boiling, salted water for 10 minutes, or until they are barely tender. Drain the beans, plunge them into cold water, then drain again. Toss them on crumpled paper towels and set aside to cool.

Grease a frying pan with 1 tablespoon of the oil. Fry the peanuts for 5 minutes over moderate heat, stirring frequently.

Cool the nuts then grind them in a blender with the remaining three tablespoons of oil, the vinegar, onion, garlic, chilli powder and sugar.

Toss together the beans, leeks, tomatoes and celery. Pour on the oil and lemon juice and season with pepper. Toss well.

Serve the sauce separately.

COOK'S TIP

Any green bean may be used in this salad, including the yellow variety, called wax beans in North America. Runner beans would need to be stringed before cooking.

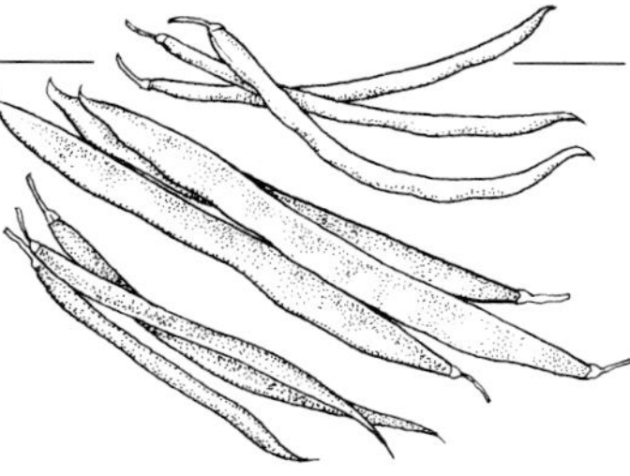

125 CHICORY AND SESAME SALAD

Preparation time:
15 minutes

Serves 4-6

Calories:
83-55 per portion

YOU WILL NEED:
3 heads of chicory
2 oranges
1 bunch of watercress
25 g/1 oz sesame seeds, toasted
4 tablespoons olive oil
1 tablespoon lemon juice
salt and pepper

Cut the chicory diagonally into 1 cm/½ inch slices and place in a bowl. Remove the peel and pith from the oranges and cut the flesh into segments, holding the fruit over the bowl so that any juice is included.

Divide the watercress into sprigs and add to the bowl with the sesame seeds.

Whisk together the oil, lemon juice, and salt and pepper to taste, then pour over the salad and toss thoroughly. Transfer to a salad bowl to serve.

COOK'S TIP

When cutting the peeled oranges into segments, cut down between the skin and flesh of each segment with a sharp knife, easing it out whole and free of skin.

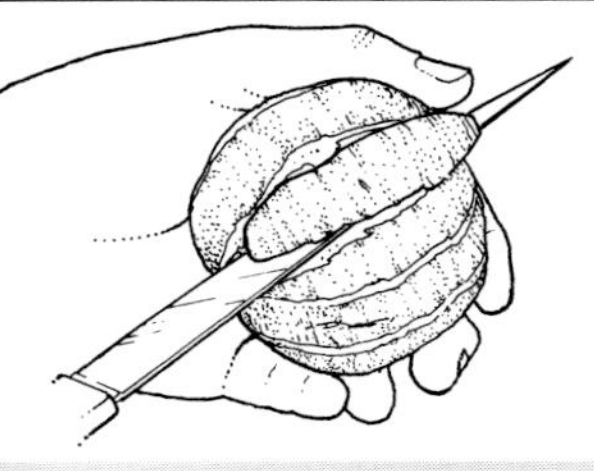

126 KOHLRABI SALAD

Preparation time:
15 minutes

Cooking time:
about 5 minutes

Serves 4

Calories:
312 per portion

YOU WILL NEED:
350 g/12 oz kohlrabi, grated
1 green pepper, cored, seeded and diced
2 celery stalks, chopped
25 g/1 oz seedless raisins
4 tablespoons vegetable oil
2 thick slices white bread, crusts removed, cut into 1 cm/½ inch cubes
FOR THE DRESSING
1 tablespoon malt vinegar
3 tablespoons vegetable oil
1 tablespoon crunchy peanut butter
1 tablespoon tomato ketchup
salt and pepper

Put the kohlrabi, pepper, celery and raisins into a bowl and stir well to mix.

Heat the oil in a frying pan, add the bread cubes and fry for about 5 minutes until crisp. Drain on kitchen paper and set aside. Place all the dressing ingredients in a screw-top jar and shake well to blend thoroughly. Pour the dressing over the salad and toss well to mix.

Just before serving, mix in a few of the croûtons and sprinkle the remainder over the top of the salad.

COOK'S TIP

To vary this salad, replace the green pepper with diced cucumber and the croûtons with salted peanuts.

127 PARSLEY, SORREL AND RADISH SALAD

Preparation time:
20 minutes

Serves 4-6

Calories:
172-115 per portion

YOU WILL NEED:
1 large bunch fresh parsley, finely chopped
24 medium sorrel leaves, coarsely chopped
4-6 sprigs fresh coriander leaves, coarsely chopped
12 medium radishes, halved
100 g/4 oz anchovy-stuffed olives
FOR THE DRESSING
4 tablespoons olive oil
1 tablespoon red wine vinegar
1 teaspoon Dijon mustard
1 teaspoon brown sugar
2 teaspoons orange juice
salt and pepper

Put the parsley, sorrel, coriander, radishes and olives into a large salad bowl.

Combine all the dressing ingredients until thoroughly mixed, then pour into the bowl. Toss the salad until it glistens all over. Serve it as soon as possible after preparing it.

COOK'S TIP

If anchovy-stuffed olives are not available, use anchovy fillet which has been pounded to a paste, and add it to the dressing. There is no substitute for the sorrel in this recipe, so leave it out if it is unavailable.

128 MIXED SPRING SALAD WITH HERB DRESSING

Preparation time:
15 minutes, plus standing

Serves 4

Calories:
358 per portion

YOU WILL NEED:
3 tablespoons finely chopped mixed fresh herbs (see Cook's Tip)
6 tablespoons French dressing (see recipe 233)
1 garlic clove, crushed
salt and pepper
1 lettuce, washed
1 bunch watercress, cleaned and trimmed
4 spring onions, washed and diced
spring onions, cleaned and trimmed, to garnish

Mix together the herbs, dressing, garlic and seasoning to taste. Leave to stand for 2 hours. In a large mixing bowl mix together the shredded lettuce, watercress and spring onions. Pour over the dressing and serve garnished with the whole spring onions.

COOK'S TIP

Choose 3 or 4 leafy herbs for this salad, such as broad-leaved parsley, tarragon, basil, marjoram, lovage or savory.

129 SPINACH VINAIGRETTE

Preparation time:
15 minutes

Cooking time:
5 minutes

Serves 4

Calories:
235 per portion

YOU WILL NEED:
750 g/1 ½ lb young spinach
salt
40 g/1 ½ oz pine nuts, or blanched slivered almonds
1 small onion, thinly sliced into rings
lemon slices, to serve
FOR THE DRESSING
4 tablespoons olive oil
1 tablespoon lemon juice
2 tablespoons chopped mint
freshly ground black pepper
½ teaspoon soft light brown sugar

Wash the spinach and cook in the water clinging to the leaves in a large pan for 5 minutes or until tender. Drain in a colander, gently pressing out the water without damaging any of the leaves.

Mix all the dressing ingredients together.

Mix the spinach in the dressing and stir in the pine nuts. Serve just warm or cool – but not chilled.

Garnish with the onion rings, if liked, and serve with lemon slices.

COOK'S TIP

Pine nuts, also called pine kernels, are delicious raw or toasted and have a particular affinity with spinach and, indeed, most salad greens.

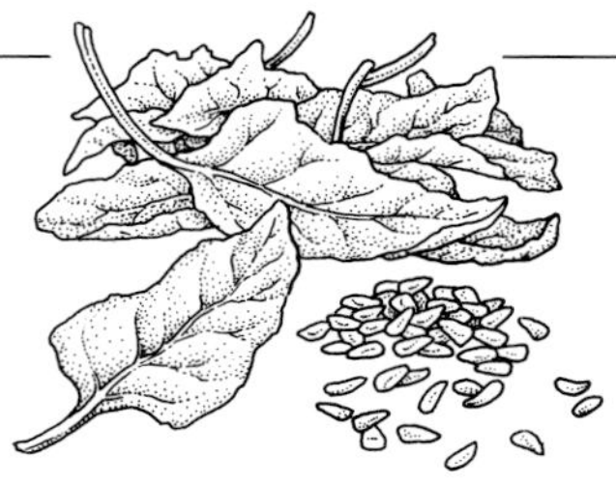

130 ARTICHOKE VINAIGRETTE

Preparation time:
4-6 minutes

Serves 4-6

Calories:
304-203 per portion

YOU WILL NEED:
450 g/1 lb Jerusalem artichokes, scrubbed
4 tablespoons French dressing (see recipe 233)
1 tablespoon chopped parsley
1 tablespoon pumpkin seeds
1 teaspoon lemon juice

Grate the artichokes coarsely and place them in a mixing bowl with the remaining ingredients. Toss thoroughly and leave the salad to marinate for 1 hour. Transfer to a shallow serving dish to serve.

COOK'S TIP

Jerusalem artichokes are members of the sunflower family and have an affinity with sunflower oil: try replacing about one-third of the olive oil in the French dressing with sunflower oil. Toss the artichokes in the dressing as soon as they are grated to prevent them discolouring.

131 POTATO AND MINT VINAIGRETTE

Preparation time:
10 minutes

Cooking time:
15 minutes

Serves 4

Calories:
293 per portion

YOU WILL NEED:
450 g/1 lb new potatoes
salt
3 tablespoons French dressing (see recipe 233)
3 tablespoons chopped mint
1 bunch radishes, thinly sliced

Cook the potatoes in their skins in boiling salted water until tender. Drain well and mix with the dressing while still warm, then leave to cool.

Add the chopped mint and radishes and mix well. Transfer to a salad bowl to serve.

COOK'S TIP

For Potato and onion vinaigrette, omit the mint and radishes and replace them with 6 chopped spring onions.

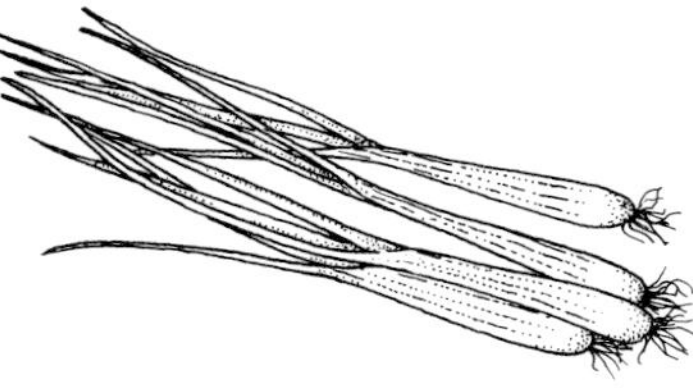

132 POTATO AND RADISH VINAIGRETTE

Preparation time:
10 minutes, plus cooling

Cooking time:
about 10 minutes

Serves 4

Calories:
395 per portion

YOU WILL NEED:
450 g/1 lb small new potatoes
salt
4 tablespoons Vinaigrette dressing (see recipe 225)
4 spring onions, sliced
1 bunch of radishes, thinly sliced

Scrub the potatoes clean but leave the skins on. Cook in boiling salted water until tender. Drain well and mix with the dressing while still warm. Leave to cool.

Add the spring onions and radishes, mix well and transfer to a salad bowl to serve.

COOK'S TIP

Potatoes cooked in their skin are an ideal wholefood. The skins provide dietary fibre and as many vitamins as possible are retained.

MAIN COURSE SALADS

Here are salads to make satisfying main course dishes all year round and for many occasions, from outdoor picnics in summer to winter suppers at home.

133 CURRIED CHICKEN MAYONNAISE

Preparation time:
10-15 minutes, plus cooling

Cooking time:
about 30 minutes

Serves 4

Calories:
977 per portion

YOU WILL NEED:
1 tablespoon olive oil
1 onion, finely chopped
½ teaspoon ground turmeric
2 teaspoons mild curry powder
2 teaspoons lemon juice
1 teaspoon apricot jam
2 tablespoons red wine
300 ml/½ pint thick Mayonnaise (see recipe 219)
500 g/18 oz cold poached chicken, cut into pieces
salt and pepper
FOR THE GARNISH
finely chopped fresh coriander
½ avocado, peeled, sliced and dipped in lemon juice

Heat the oil in a frying pan. Add the onion and fry over a gentle heat for 5 minutes until soft and lightly coloured. Stir in the turmeric and curry powder. Cook for a further 2 minutes. Add the lemon juice, jam and wine and simmer for 20 minutes. Remove from the heat and leave to cool for 5 minutes.

Put the mayonnaise in a large bowl and add the curry mixture, stirring very thoroughly to mix. Add the chicken and turn in the curried mayonnaise until thoroughly coated. Garnish with chopped coriander and avocado slices.

COOK'S TIP

Use the other half of the avocado to make a dip with soured cream and lemon juice. Add salt and pepper to taste. Cover with cling film and chill before serving.

134 CHICKEN SALAD WITH SWEETCORN

Preparation time:
20 minutes

Cooking time:
20-25 minutes

Serves 4

Calories:
651 per portion

YOU WILL NEED:
1 tablespoon plain flour, seasoned salt and pepper
4 chicken pieces
1 egg, beaten
50 g/2 oz fresh white breadcrumbs
50 g/2 oz butter
1 tablespoon vegetable oil
450 g/1 lb frozen sweetcorn kernels
4 small bananas
4 kumquats, sliced, to garnish
dressing, to serve (see Cook's Tip)

Dust the flour over the chicken pieces. Dip the chicken first in the beaten egg, then in the breadcrumbs, pressing on well.

Heat the butter and oil in a large frying pan, add the chicken pieces and fry gently for 15-20 minutes, until browned all over and cooked. Drain on absorbent kitchen paper.

Meanwhile, cook the sweetcorn in a saucepan of boiling salted water until tender. Drain and leave to cool.

Peel the bananas and cut in half lengthways. Heat the oil remaining in the pan, add the bananas and fry quickly for about 3 minutes, turning once, until lightly browned. Drain and cool.

Beat the soured cream into a bowl. Stir in the vinegar and season to taste.

Arrange the chicken pieces on a platter and surround with the sweetcorn and fried bananas. Garnish with the kumquat slices. Hand the dressing separately.

COOK'S TIP

For a tangy dressing for this salad, beat together in a bowl 300 ml/½ pint soured cream, 2 tablespoons white wine vinegar or lemon juice and salt and pepper to taste.

135 CHICKEN AND WALNUT SALAD

Preparation time:
20 minutes

Serves 4

Calories:
442 per portion

YOU WILL NEED:
450 g/1 lb cooked boned chicken
2 celery sticks, coarsely chopped
1 large dessert apple, cored and diced
50 g/2 oz walnuts, roughly chopped
6 tablespoons Mayonnaise (see recipe 219)
1-2 tablespoons single cream (optional)
watercress sprigs, to garnish

Cut the chicken into pieces and place in a large bowl with the celery, apple and walnuts.

Thin the mayonnaise if necessary to give the consistency of thick cream, by adding a little single cream. Pour over the chicken and toss well until the ingredients are evenly coated.

Turn into a serving dish and garnish with watercress.

COOK'S TIP

Cooked boned turkey can replace the chicken in this rich salad. Many supermarkets now sell turkey portions throughout the year.

136 MIDSUMMER CHICKEN

Preparation time:
30 minutes, plus marinating

Serves 4

Calories:
426 per portion

YOU WILL NEED:
450 g/1 lb cooked chicken meat, skinned and boned
5 tablespoons dry white wine
1 teaspoon lemon juice
2 teaspoons grated onion
1 teaspoon chopped fresh tarragon
pinch of onion salt
4 oranges, peeled and segmented
100 g/4 oz lamb's lettuce
1 bunch watercress
50 g/2 oz toasted pine nuts or walnuts
blanched julienne strips of orange rind
FOR THE DRESSING
75 g/3 oz full-fat soft cheese
150 ml/¼ pint soured cream
3 drops Tabasco sauce
salt and pepper

Cut the chicken into thin strips. Place in a bowl with the wine, lemon juice, onion, tarragon, onion salt and orange segments, blending well. Cover and leave to marinate for 20 minutes. Meanwhile toss the lamb's lettuce with the watercress and use to line a serving dish.

Remove the chicken and orange segments from the marinade and mix with the pine nuts or walnuts, reserving the marinade. Spoon the mixture on to the lettuce.

Blend the cheese with the soured cream, Tabasco and salt and pepper to taste. Add sufficient marinade to make a thick pouring consistency. Pour over the chicken mixture. Sprinkle a few julienne strips of orange rind over the chicken mixture.

COOK'S TIP

Use a potato peeler to remove narrow strips of rind before peeling the oranges, carefully avoiding the pith. Blanch in boiling water for 2-3 minutes.

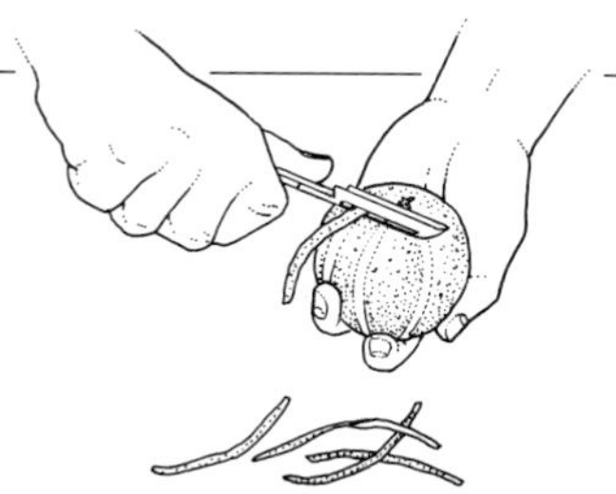

137 WEST INDIAN CHICKEN SALAD

Preparation time:
35 minutes

Serves 6

Calories:
486 per portion

YOU WILL NEED:
4 celery sticks, thinly sliced
4 slices fresh pineapple, cubed
50 g/2 oz pecan nuts
1.25 kg/2½ lb cooked chicken, skinned, boned and sliced
1 small lettuce heart, shredded
1 avocado, halved, stoned, peeled and sliced
1 tablespoon lemon juice
FOR THE DRESSING
150 ml/¼ pint natural yogurt
1 teaspoon curry powder
1 teaspoon curry paste
1 tablespoon double cream
1 tablespoon clear honey
½ teaspoon lemon juice
salt and pepper

Mix together the ingredients for the dressing, adding salt and pepper to taste.

Toss together the celery, pineapple and pecans and pour on the dressing. Stir to mix well. Add the chicken and toss carefully to avoid breaking up the meat.

Arrange the shredded lettuce in a ring around the outside of a serving dish. Toss the avocado slices in the lemon juice as soon as they are cut. Arrange them over the lettuce. Spoon the chicken salad into the centre of the serving dish.

COOK'S TIP

Try making your own blend of curry powder by combining freshly ground coriander seeds, turmeric, fenugreek, ginger, black pepper, cardamom and cinnamon. It will be far superior to the prepared varieties.

138 ITALIAN SALAD

Preparation time:
15-20 minutes

Serves 4

Calories:
168 per portion

YOU WILL NEED:
350 g/12 oz cooked chicken, turkey or veal
8 tomatoes
1 fennel bulb, roughly chopped
lettuce leaves
1 x 50 g/2 oz can anchovies, drained and rinsed

Cut the poultry or veal into bite-sized pieces.

Roughly chop 4 of the tomatoes and mix with the fennel.

Arrange the lettuce on a large platter. Slice the remaining tomatoes and place in a ring on top of the lettuce.

Mix the meat with the tomato and fennel mixture and spoon into the centre of the tomato ring. Place the anchovies in a criss-cross pattern on top of the salad. Serve with Lemon vinaigrette (see recipe 227).

COOK'S TIP

If you do not like the slightly aniseed flavour of fennel, replace the bulb with 3-4 celery sticks, roughly chopped.

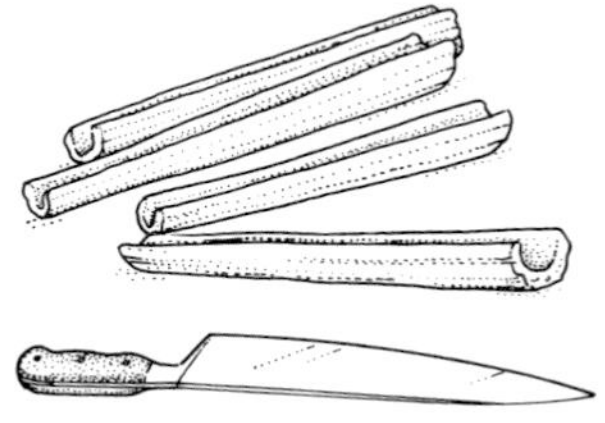

139 STUFFED FRENCH BREAD

Preparation time:
20-25 minutes

Serves 2

Calories:
681 per portion

YOU WILL NEED:
100 g/4 oz white cabbage, grated
25 g/1 oz onion, grated
1 small carrot, grated
1 celery stick, chopped
15 g/½ oz raisins
2 walnuts, coarsely chopped
3 tablespoons mayonnaise
1 crusty French bread stick
15 g/½ oz butter
2 lettuce leaves, shredded
2 slices Mortadella, rindless and rolled
25 g/1 oz salami, rindless and rolled into cornets
40 g/1½ oz smoked cheese, rindless and sliced
40 g/1½ oz blue cheese, sliced
1 hard-boiled egg, sliced
1 large beef tomato, sliced

Combine the cabbage with the onion, carrot, celery, raisins and walnuts, mixing well. Bind together with the mayonnaise.

Split the bread stick in half horizontally and butter the inside lightly. Spread the cabbage mixture along the length of the bottom half of the bread stick and top with the lettuce, Mortadella, salami, smoked cheese, blue cheese, egg and tomato, arranging attractively. Press the bread stick halves firmly together and cut vertically into 2 thick sections to serve.

COOK'S TIP

The cabbage mixture can be made in advance and stored in the refrigerator for up to 5 days. Other cold meats can replace the Mortadella and salami, if preferred.

140 SURPRISE LOAF

Preparation time:
25 minutes

Serves 4

Calories:
638 per portion

YOU WILL NEED:
500 g/18 oz cooked chicken meat
1 long stick French bread
6-10 lettuce leaves
butter, for spreading
225 g/8 oz cooked ham, finely chopped
3 hard-boiled eggs, chopped
5 tablespoons mayonnaise
3 tablespoons tomato ketchup
1 tablespoon lemon juice
salt and pepper

Skin the chicken and chop into bite-sized pieces.

Cut the French loaf in half lengthways, and scoop out the bread from the bottom half, leaving just a thin layer all round. Line the bottom half with the lettuce leaves. Lightly spread the top half of the loaf with butter.

Put the chicken, ham and hard-boiled eggs in a bowl, add the mayonnaise and tomato ketchup and mix thoroughly. Add the lemon juice, salt and pepper and mix again, then pile into the lettuce-lined bread, pressing in with the back of a spoon to level. Replace the top of the loaf and wrap tightly in foil if taking to a picnic.

COOK'S TIP

Make breadcrumbs with the scooped-out bread and reserve for another recipe. Leave them to become dry before storing unless you are using them immediately.

141 COLD TONGUE GIARDINERA

Preparation time:
15 minutes, plus marinating

Serves 4

Calories:
232 per portion

YOU WILL NEED:
100 g/4 oz frozen mixed vegetables, lightly cooked
2 pickled onions, chopped
2 gherkins, chopped
6 stuffed olives, sliced
50 g/2 oz capers, chopped
4 tablespoons French dressing (see recipe 233)
1 tablespoon white wine vinegar
350 g/2 oz cooked tongue, thinly sliced
4 hard-boiled eggs, sliced
chopped parsley, to garnish

Put the vegetables in a bowl with the pickled onions, gherkins, olives, capers, French dressing and vinegar. Leave to marinate for 4 hours.

Arrange the tongue slices on a serving dish and spoon over the vegetable mixture. Garnish with the egg slices and the chopped parsley.

COOK'S TIP

Instead of white wine vinegar, you can use 1 tablespoon of the pickling liquid from the jar of pickled onions, if preferred.

142 COLD SMOKED PORK WITH MANGO MAYONNAISE

Preparation time:
10 minutes

Serves 4

Calories:
362 per portion

YOU WILL NEED:
3 tablespoons mango chutney
6 tablespoons thick mayonnaise
salt and pepper
1 small iceberg lettuce, shredded
½ cucumber, sliced
350 g/12 oz cold smoked pork, sliced
fresh or canned, drained mango slices, to garnish (see Cook's Tip)

Stir the chutney into the mayonnaise and season to taste. Place the lettuce and cucumber in a salad bowl.

Arrange the cold pork on a serving platter and garnish with mango slices. Spoon a little of the mango mayonnaise into the centre and hand round the remainder separately in a bowl.

COOK'S TIP

To slice a fresh mango: choose fruit that is still fairly firm and peel it. Then make a cut from one tip to the other with a sharp knife. Make a second cut about 5 mm/¼ inch away and ease the slice out with the knife.

143 ROAST BEEF SALAD WITH SOURED CREAM AND OLIVES

Preparation time:
15 minutes

Serves 4

Calories:
399 per portion

YOU WILL NEED:
450 g/1 lb rare roast beef, thickly sliced
175 ml/6 fl oz soured cream
juice of 1 lemon
100 g/4 oz black olives, halved and stoned

Cut the beef slices into strips and place in a serving dish. Mix together the soured cream and lemon juice. Add half the olives to the beef slices and spoon over the cream.

Garnish with the remaining olives.

COOK'S TIP

Jacket potatoes make a good accompaniment to this salad but remember to allow enough time for them to be thoroughly cooked.

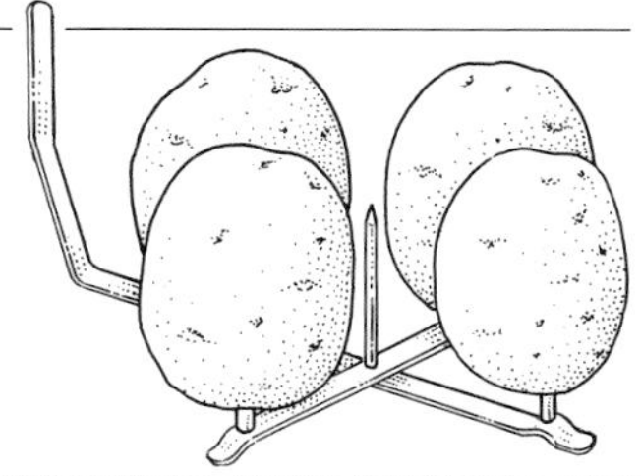

144 DUCK BREASTS WITH HONEY VINAIGRETTE

Preparation time:
15 minutes, plus cooling

Cooking time:
35 minutes

Oven temperature:
240 C/475 F/Gas 9

Serves 6

Calories:
486 per portion

YOU WILL NEED:
6 boned duck breasts
salt and pepper
1 head radicchio, shredded
1 curly endive, shredded
FOR THE VINAIGRETTE
4 ½ tablespoons lemon juice
1 ½ teaspoons Dijon mustard
1 garlic clove, finely chopped
1 ½ tablespoons clear honey
175 ml/6 fl oz olive oil

Prick the skin on the duck breasts all over with a fork, then rub generously with salt and pepper. Place the ducks on a grid in a roasting tin and cook in a preheated oven for 20 minutes, then turn off the heat. Cover the breasts with foil and leave them for another 15 minutes to finish cooking, with the oven door ajar. When cool, slice the breasts lengthways at a slight angle, not quite cutting through at one end.

To make the vinaigrette, whisk together the lemon juice and mustard, then add the garlic, honey and 1 tablespoon of the oil and whisk until beginning to thicken. Add the remaining oil, a little at a time, constantly whisking until the mixture is thick and fluffy. Season with salt and pepper.

Lay the radicchio down one side of a serving platter, the curly endive down the other, and put the duck breasts, slightly fanned out, down the middle. Pour some vinaigrette over the duck breasts, reserving a little for the accompanying salads.

COOK'S TIP

This salad is also excellent picnic fare and can easily be assembled in the chosen place. Transport the vinaigrette in a screw-top jar and shake well before using.

145 POTATO SALAD WITH LOBSTER, HAM AND TRUFFLE

Preparation time:
20 minutes, plus standing

Serves 4

Calories:
366 per portion

YOU WILL NEED:
450 g/1 lb waxy potatoes, cooked in their skins, peeled and sliced
1 lobster tail, peeled and thinly sliced
1 thick slice cooked ham, about 75 g/3 oz
2 canned pimientos, drained and diced
1 x 25 g/1 oz jar chopped truffles or 1 x 15 g/½ oz can whole truffles
FOR THE DRESSING
6 tablespoons olive oil
3 tablespoons lemon juice
salt and pepper

Combine the potatoes, lobster, ham, pimiento and truffles in a large salad bowl, mixing lightly with two forks.

Thoroughly combine the dressing ingredients and pour over the salad. Toss lightly to coat all the ingredients in the dressing. Leave to stand at room temperature for 30 minutes before serving, to allow the aroma of the truffles to penetrate the other ingredients.

COOK'S TIP

This elegant and luxurious salad is a perfect main course for a celebration lunch in midsummer and needs no accompaniments other than an appropriately fine wine.

146 PRAWN, MANGETOUT AND HAZELNUT SALAD

Preparation time:
10 minutes, plus cooling

Cooking time:
8-9 minutes

Serves 2

Calories:
460 per portion

YOU WILL NEED:
225 g/8 oz mangetout or stringless French beans, topped and tailed
100 g/4 oz peeled cooked prawns, defrosted if frozen
50 g/2 oz hazelnuts, whole or halved, skins removed and lightly toasted, to garnish
FOR THE DRESSING
3 tablespoons olive oil or 2 tablespoons olive and 1 tablespoon walnut oil
2 tablespoons lemon juice
salt and pepper

Put the mangetout or beans in a double boiler or steamer, cover and steam for about 6 minutes. Add the prawns and steam for a further 2-3 minutes until the prawns are heated through and the mangetout barely tender.

Turn the mangetout and prawns into a dish. Thoroughly combine the ingredients for the dressing and spoon over the salad, tossing gently to mix. Leave to cool for at least 2 hours.

Just before serving, sprinkle with the hazelnuts and a twist or two of black pepper.

COOK'S TIP

This salad is best served at room temperature, accompanied by thin slices of brown bread and butter and a glass of dry white wine.

147 COURGETTE AND SALMON SURPRISE

Preparation time:
25 minutes, plus standing

Serves 4

Calories:
169 per portion

YOU WILL NEED:
225 g/8 oz courgettes, thinly sliced diagonally
100 g/4 oz button mushrooms, thinly sliced
1 shallot, thinly sliced into rings
1 head chicory, leaves separated
100 g/4 oz smoked salmon, cut into matchstick strips
1 lemon, quartered, to serve
FOR THE DRESSING
3 tablespoons olive oil
1 teaspoon grated lemon rind
1 tablespoon lemon juice
pepper
cayenne
1 tablespoon finely snipped chives

Mix together the ingredients for the dressing. Toss together the courgettes, mushrooms and shallot. Add the dressing and toss again. Leave at room temperature for about 30 minutes.

Line a serving dish with the chicory leaves. Spoon the courgette and mushroom salad on top and arrange the smoked salmon strips in the centre. Serve with lemon wedges.

COOK'S TIP

You may find it easier to cut the smoked salmon into neat matchstick strips if you use a pair of sharp kitchen scissors.

148 PAPAYA PRAWNS

Preparation time:
20 minutes

Serves 4

Calories:
198 per portion

YOU WILL NEED:
4 large papayas, about 225 g/8 oz each
2 teaspoons fresh lime juice
8 large peeled cooked king prawns, chopped
1 red pepper, cored, seeded and chopped
6 tablespoons Mayonnaise
2 teaspoons freshly grated horseradish
finely grated rind of 1 lime
FOR THE GARNISH
twists of lime
few whole unpeeled cooked prawns (optional)

Cut the papayas in half lengthways, scoop and discard the seeds. Carefully scoop out the flesh with a melon baller or cut into small cubes, leaving the shells intact. Mix the papaya flesh with the remaining ingredients, blending well. Spoon the papaya mixture back into the reserved shells. Place two shells on each of 4 individual serving plates.

Chill lightly before serving garnished with twists of lime and a few unpeeled prawns (if used).

COOK'S TIP

A papaya resembles an elongated melon and is ripe when the skin turns yellow and feels tender when lightly pressed, especially at the stalk end of the fruit.

149 ITALIAN SEAFOOD SALAD

Preparation time:
20-25 minutes

Cooking time:
3 minutes

Serves 4

Calories:
262 per portion

YOU WILL NEED:
450 g/1 lb cooked white fish fillets, such as plaice, skinned and cut into 5 cm/ 2 inch slices
100 g/4 oz peeled cooked prawns
1 x 40 g/1½ oz can anchovy fillets, drained and chopped
4 tablespoons black olives
2 tablespoons chopped fennel or parsley
salad leaves
FOR THE DRESSING
3 tablespoons sunflower oilp
6 tablespoons dry white wine
1 tablespoon lemon juice
1 small onion or shallot, chopped
1 garlic clove, crushed
1 red pepper, cored, seeded and chopped
salt and pepper

Put all the ingredients for the dressing into a saucepan and bring to the boil. Leave to cool.

Carefully toss together the white fish, prawns, anchovies, olives and herb. Pour on the cooled dressing and stir gently, taking care not to break up the fish.

Line a serving dish with salad leaves. Spoon the fish mixture on top.

COOK'S TIP

Remember to add very little salt to the dressing as there are anchovies in this salad. Rinse the olives in cold water if they have been bottled in brine.

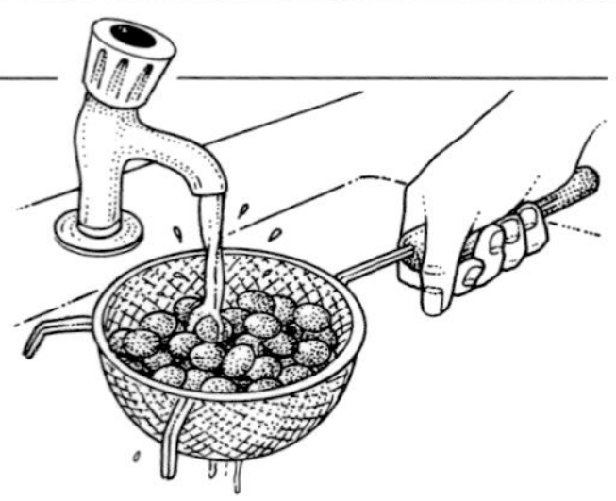

150 SEAFOOD AND ASPARAGUS

Preparation time:
10 minutes

Cooking time:
10-15 minutes

Serves 4

Calories
103 per portion

YOU WILL NEED:
225 g/8 oz cod
8 fresh asparagus stalks
lettuce leaves
100 g/4 oz peeled cooked prawns
1 x 100 g/4 oz can mussels, drained
chopped fresh dill, to garnish

Poach the cod in the minimum of water for 10-15 minutes. Drain, cool and flake with a fork.

Meanwhile cook the asparagus.

Line a salad bowl with lettuce leaves and arrange the prawns, mussels and asparagus round the edge.

Place the cod in the centre and sprinkle with chopped dill.

COOK'S TIP

When asparagus is out of season and only available at inflated prices, you can use 1 x 225 g/8 oz can asparagus spears, drained.

151 HALIBUT SALAD

Preparation time:
15-20 minutes

Cooking time:
35 minutes

Oven temperature:
180 C/350 F/Gas 4

Serves 4

Calories:
277 per portion

YOU WILL NEED:
575 g/1¼ lb halibut
4 tablespoons olive oil
2 tablespoons lemon juice
salt and pepper
1 bunch spring onions
4 tablespoons chopped mixed herbs: tarragon, chervil, chives and dill

Brush a piece of foil with 1 tablespoon of the olive oil and lay the fish on it. Sprinkle the fish with 1 tablespoon of the lemon juice and some salt and pepper. Wrap up the fish in the foil and lay on a rack in a roasting tin. Bake in a preheated oven for 35 minutes. When it is cooked, allow the fish to cool before unwrapping it.

Break the fish into large flakes, discarding the skin and bone, and put it into a bowl. Mix the fish very gently with the remaining oil and lemon juice. Slice the spring onions and add them to the fish. Try not to break up the fish more than you can help. Add plenty of salt and pepper and stir in the chopped herbs.

Serve with tomato, rice and green salads for a satisfying summer meal.

COOK'S TIP

If possible, choose one thick piece of halibut weighing 575 g/1¼ lb. Use the discarded skin and bone to make some fish stock for another recipe.

152 SHELLFISH SALAD

Preparation time:
25-30 minutes

Cooking time:
20-25 minutes

Serves 4

Calories:
381 per portion

YOU WILL NEED:
450 g/1 lb hake or halibut
juice of 2 lemons
6 scallops
6 peeled cooked giant prawns
225 g/8 oz peeled cooked prawns
1 green pepper, cored and seeded
½ cucumber, peeled
1 cos lettuce, shredded
4 hard-boiled eggs
herb sauce (see Cook's Tip below)

Put the hake or halibut in a large saucepan and just cover with cold water. Bring to the boil and poach gently until the fish is cooked. Remove the pan from the heat and allow the fish to cool in the cooking liquor. When cool, drain the fish, remove all skin and bone and break the flesh into large flakes. Pour the juice of 1 lemon over the fish and set it aside while preparing the other ingredients.

Poach the prepared scallops for 4-5 minutes in the same water as the fish. Drain them, discarding the liquor, moisten with lemon juice and set aside. Soak the prawns for 10 minutes in cold, slightly salty water. Cut the green pepper and cucumber into sticks like thin matchsticks. Cut the scallops into slices.

Put the shredded lettuce in a large bowl and cover with the green pepper and the cucumber. Pile the flaked hake or halibut in the centre, and surround with the halved, hard-boiled eggs. Scatter the prawns and sliced scallops on top. Pour the herb sauce over the salad and mix well before serving.

COOK'S TIP

To make the herb sauce, purée 100 g/4 oz medium-fat cream cheese and 150 ml/¼ pint buttermilk together in a blender, adding a drop of lemon juice and salt and pepper to taste. Stir in 3 tablespoons chopped fresh tarragon.

153 SMOKED MACKEREL SALAD

Preparation time:
15 minutes, plus draining

Serves 4

Calories:
301 per portion

YOU WILL NEED:
1 cucumber, thinly sliced
salt
1 head chicory
lettuce leaves
4 hard-boiled eggs, sliced
350 g/12 oz smoked mackerel, flaked
1 garlic clove, crushed

Place the cucumber on a plate, sprinkle with salt and cover with a second plate. Press down with a weight and leave for 30 minutes.

Arrange the chicory and lettuce leaves in a shallow bowl. Place the cucumber slices round the edge. Arrange the egg slices next to the cucumber and the flaked mackerel in the centre.

Stir the crushed garlic into a Lemon vinaigrette (see recipe 227) and serve with the salad.

COOK'S TIP

A simple tomato side salad goes well with the smoked mackerel and hard-boiled eggs and adds a colourful touch.

154 GOLDEN SALAD

Preparation time:
20 minutes

Serves 4

Calories:
445 per portion

YOU WILL NEED:
4 smoked mackerel fillets
2 large oranges, peeled and segmented
2 dessert apples, cored and thinly sliced
2 tender celery sticks, thinly sliced
2 tablespoons walnut halves
curly endive or lettuce leaves
4 thin orange slices, to garnish
FOR THE DRESSING
1 teaspoon grated orange rind
3 tablespoons orange juice
2 tablespoons tomato juice
large pinch of cayenne pepper
1 tablespoon clear honey
2 tablespoons finely snipped chives

Skin the mackerel fillets and cut each one into 4 pieces.

Mix together the dressing ingredients. Toss the orange segments, apples, celery and walnuts in the dressing. Carefully stir in the piece of mackerel.

Line a plate with salad leaves and spoon on the salad. Garnish with the orange slices.

COOK'S TIP

The unusual combination of orange and tomato in the dressing complements the varied ingredients of the salad. This dressing is also good served with white fish.

155 CAULIFLOWER ITALIANO

Preparation time:
10 minutes

Cooking time:
about 20 minutes

Serves 4

Calories:
65 per portion

YOU WILL NEED:
2 tablespoons French dressing (see recipe 233)
1 tablespoon onion, finely chopped
1 garlic clove, crushed
1 cauliflower, broken into florets
2 tablespoons finely chopped green pepper
6 small tomatoes, skinned
salt
dried basil

Pour the salad dressing into a deep frying pan and cook the onion and garlic in it until tender. Add the cauliflower with 3 tablespoons water. Cook, covered, over a low heat for about 10 minutes until the cauliflower is cooked but still crisp. Add the chopped pepper and cook for a further 5 minutes. Stir in the whole tomatoes and heat through. Add salt and dried basil to taste and serve.

156 FENNEL, APPLE AND WALNUT SALAD

Preparation time:
15 minutes

Serves 4

Calories:
470 per portion

YOU WILL NEED:
2 small heads fennel, about 225 g/8 oz each, halved lengthways
4 small dessert apples, quartered, cored and thinly sliced
50 g/2 oz walnuts, coarsely chopped
FOR THE DRESSING
150 ml/¼ pint thick mayonnaise
5 tablespoons fresh orange juice
salt and pepper

Trim the feathery green leaves from the fennel tops and reserve for the garnish. Slice the fennel very finely and place in a large bowl. Add the apples and nuts and stir well to mix.

Put the mayonnaise in a bowl, add the orange juice and beat until smooth and thoroughly blended. Season to taste. Pour the dressing over the salad and toss until all the ingredients are thoroughly coated. Garnish with the reserved fennel leaves.

COOK'S TIP

Serve this unusual salad on a chilly day with some hot crusty bread. Replace some of the white cauliflower with the pretty green cauliflower, if available.

COOK'S TIP

Try replacing the fennel with celery and the walnuts with cashew nuts or hazelnuts for a variation of this deliciously crunchy salad.

PULSES, PASTAS & GRAINS

In this chapter, some of the world's oldest and most valuable staple foods form the basis of salads rich in protein and fibre and absolutely delicious, too.

157 HUMMOUS

Preparation time:
10 minutes, plus cooling

Cooking time:
2-2½ hours

Serves 4

Calories
212 per portion

YOU WILL NEED:
100 g/4 oz chick peas, soaked overnight
salt and pepper
2 tablespoons tahini
1-2 garlic cloves, crushed
juice of ½ lemon
2 tablespoons olive oil
few lettuce leaves
2 teaspoons chopped mint

Drain the chick peas, place in a pan and cover with cold water. Bring to the boil, boil rapidly for 10 minutes then simmer gently for 2-2½ hours until soft, adding a little salt towards the end of the cooking.

Drain, reserving 120 ml/4 fl oz of the liquid. Place the chick peas in an electric blender with the tahini, garlic, lemon juice, oil, reserved liquid, ½ teaspoon salt and ¼ teaspoon pepper. Blend to a soft creamy purée; check the seasoning.

Arrange on a bed of lettuce and sprinkle with the mint. Serve with crusty bread or warm pitta bread.

COOK'S TIP

This classic dish from the eastern Mediterranean becomes an excellent starter salad dip when served with crudités.

158 MIXED BEAN SALAD

Preparation time:
10 minutes, plus soaking overnight

Cooking time:
1-1½ hours

Serves 8

Calories:
184 per portion

YOU WILL NEED:
100 g/4 oz butter beans
100 g/4 oz red kidney beans
100 g/4 oz haricot beans
salt
100 g/4 oz French beans, cut into 2.5 cm/1 inch lengths
6 spring onions, chopped
4 tablespoons French dressing (see recipe 233)
2 tablespoons chopped parsley

Soak the beans separately overnight. Drain and place in separate pans. Cover with cold water, bring to the boil, boil rapidly for 10 minutes then simmer for 1-1½ hours, adding a little salt towards the end of cooking; drain.

Cook the French beans in boiling salted water for 7-8 minutes; drain. Place all the beans in a bowl and mix in the onions and dressing while still warm. Leave to cool.

Stir in the parsley and transfer to a salad bowl to serve.

COOK'S TIP

This is an excellent picnic salad, since it transports well in a lidded plastic box. It also benefits from being given plenty of time for the beans to absorb the dressing.

159 ADUKI BEAN SALAD

Preparation time:
15 minutes, plus cooling

Cooking time:
40-45 minutes

Serves 4

Calories:
313 per portion

YOU WILL NEED:
225 g/8 oz aduki beans, soaked overnight
salt and pepper
6 tablespoons Ginger dressing (see recipe 234)
6 spring onions, chopped
4 tomatoes, skinned and chopped
3 celery sticks, sliced
2 tablespoons chopped parsley

Drain the beans, place in a pan of boiling salted water and boil rapidly for 10 minutes. Cover and cook for 30-35 minutes or until tender. Drain well and mix with the dressing while still warm. Leave to cool.

Add the remaining ingredients, seasoning with salt and pepper to taste. Mix thoroughly and transfer to a shallow dish to serve.

COOK'S TIP

Aduki beans are a small, red bean with a sweet but quite strong flavour. They are native to China. Red kidney beans, though bigger, make a suitable substitute.

160 FLAGEOLET VINAIGRETTE

Preparation time:
15 minutes, plus cooling

Cooking time:
about 1 hour 15 minutes

Serves 4

Calories:
386 per portion

YOU WILL NEED:
225 g/8 oz flageolet beans, soaked overnight
salt
6 tablespoons French dressing (see recipe 233)
1 red pepper, cored, seeded and chopped (see Cook's Tip)
4 spring onions, chopped
1 tablespoon chopped mixed herbs: parsley, thyme and mint
2 celery sticks, thinly sliced

Drain the beans, place in a pan and cover with cold water. Bring to the boil and boil rapidly for 10 minutes then simmer for about 1 hour, until tender, adding a little salt towards the end of the cooking. Drain thoroughly and place in a bowl.

Pour the dressing over the beans while they are still warm and mix well. Leave to cool, then add the remaining ingredients. Toss thoroughly and transfer to a shallow dish to serve.

COOK'S TIP

Peppers may be more easily digested if they are skinned before use: put the whole pepper under a hot grill for a few minutes, turning frequently, until the outer skin is slightly charred. It can then be peeled off.

161 BUTTER BEAN VINAIGRETTE

Preparation time:
10 minutes, plus cooling

Cooking time:
1-1¼ hours

Serves 4

Calories:
305 per portion

YOU WILL NEED:
225 g/8 oz butter beans, soaked overnight
salt
4 tablespoons Vinaigrette dressing (see recipe 225)
4 spring onions, chopped
1 garlic clove, crushed
1 tablespoon chopped parsley, to garnish

Drain the beans, place in a pan and cover with cold water. Bring to the boil, boil rapidly for 10 minutes then simmer gently for 1-1¼ hours, adding a little salt towards the end of the cooking; drain.

Mix with the dressing while the beans are still warm. Add the onions and garlic and mix well. Transfer to a serving dish and leave until cold. Sprinkle with the parsley to serve.

COOK'S TIP

Make this salad very quickly by using a large can of butter beans. They will need no cooking. Drain well before using them.

162 BUTTER BEAN AND CAULIFLOWER SALAD

Preparation time:
10 minutes, plus cooling

Cooking time:
about 1 hour

Serves 6-8

Calories:
50-38 per portion

YOU WILL NEED:
100 g/4 oz butter beans, soaked overnight
salt
1 small cauliflower, broken into florets
100 g/4 oz button mushrooms, sliced
6 tablespoons Green herb dressing (see recipe 236)

Drain the beans, place in a pan and cover with cold water. Bring to the boil and simmer for 1 hour or until softened, adding a little salt towards the end of the cooking. Drain and cool.

Cook the cauliflower in boiling salted water for 3 minutes; drain and cool.

Place the beans, cauliflower and mushrooms in a salad bowl. Add the dressing and toss well. Serve immediately.

COOK'S TIP

This is another salad in which using canned beans is a great time saver. Instead of butter beans, try the smaller borlotti beans or red kidney beans, both available canned.

163 TUNA AND BEAN SALAD

Preparation time:
00 minutes

Serves 4

Calories:
278 per portion

YOU WILL NEED:
1 x 100 g/4 oz can and 1 x 198 g/7 oz can tuna fish, drained and flaked
1 x 439 g/15½ oz can butter beans, drained
4 tablespoons French dressing (see recipe 233)
chopped capers, to garnish

Mix the tuna and butter beans together. Pour over the French dressing and toss well to coat.

Turn into a serving dish and garnish with capers.

164 THREE BEAN SALAD

Preparation time:
10 minutes

Serves 4

Calories:
331 per portion

YOU WILL NEED:
225 g/8 oz cooked chick peas
225 g/8 oz cooked red kidney beans
225 g/8 oz cooked green beans
2 teaspoons chopped fresh mixed herbs or 1 teaspoon dried mixed herbs
6-8 tablespoons Lemon vinaigrette (see recipe 227)

Mix the chick peas and red kidney beans together in a salad bowl.

Cut the green beans into short pieces and add to the bean mixture.

Sprinkle with the herbs. Add the Lemon vinaigrette and mix well.

COOK'S TIP

Use tuna fish in brine, since there is already oil in the French dressing. A few finely sliced rings of raw onion would add an extra tang to this salad.

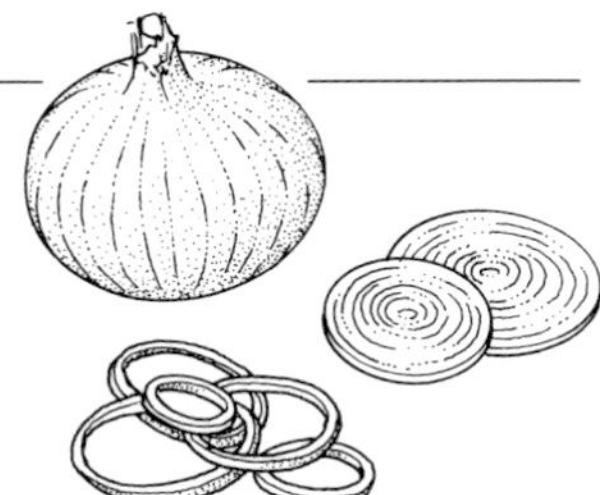

COOK'S TIP

For a really quick-to-prepare salad, use canned chick peas and red kidney beans, draining them well before use.

165 RED BEAN AND BEANSHOOT SALAD

Preparation time:
10 minutes, plus cooling

Cooking time:
about 1 hour

Serves 4

Calories:
334 per portion

YOU WILL NEED:
175 g/6 oz red kidney beans, soaked overnight
salt
100 g/4 oz mushrooms, sliced
6 tablespoons Vinaigrette dressing (see recipe 225)
225 g/8 oz beanshoots
1 red pepper, cored, seeded and thinly sliced
2 tablespoons toasted sunflower seeds
2 tablespoons chopped parsley

Drain the beans, place in a pan and cover with cold water. Bring to the boil, cover and boil rapidly for 10 minutes, then simmer for 45-60 minutes, until tender; add a little salt towards the end of the cooking.

Drain the beans and place in a bowl with the mushrooms. Pour over the dressing and mix thoroughly. Leave to cool.

Add the remaining ingredients and toss well. Transfer to a shallow dish to serve.

COOK'S TIP

Dried kidney beans should be fast-boiled for ten minutes before being simmered until cooked to ensure that potentially harmful toxins are destroyed.

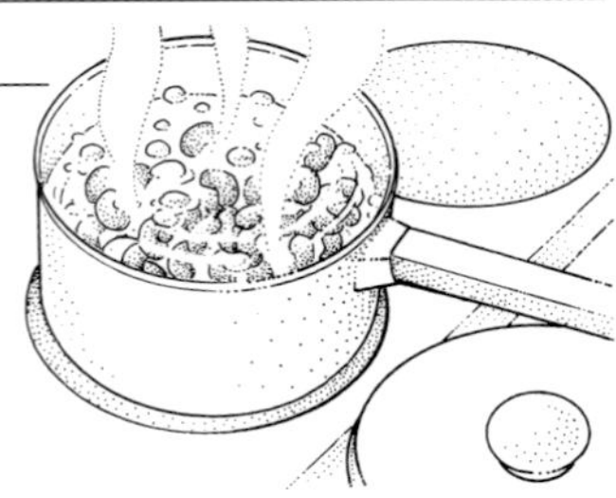

166 SEAFOOD PASTA

Preparation time:
30 minutes

Cooking time:
about 10 minutes

Serves 4

Calories:
407 per portion

YOU WILL NEED:
175 g/6 oz pasta twists (fusilli)
1 avocado, peeled, stoned and sliced
2 teaspoons lemon juice
175 g/6 oz peeled prawns
1 x 200 g/7 oz jar mussels in brine, rinsed and drained
3 tomatoes, cut into wedges
50 g/2 oz button mushrooms, sliced
FOR THE DRESSING
2 tablespoons mayonnaise
2 tablespoons soured cream
3/4-1 teaspoon garlic purée
2 teaspoons snipped chives
salt and pepper
few whole unpeeled prawns, to garnish

Cook the pasta twists in boiling salted water according to the packet instructions, for about 8-10 minutes. Drain and allow to cool.

In a bowl, toss the avocado slices in the lemon juice and add the pasta with the prawns, mussels, tomatoes and mushrooms, mixing gently.

Mix the mayonnaise with the soured cream, garlic purée, chives and salt and pepper to taste. (This dressing can be stored tightly covered in the refrigerator for up to 3 days. Stir well before using.)

Fold the dressing into the salad and spoon into a serving dish. Chill lightly then garnish with prawns.

COOK'S TIP

Try other pasta shapes in this salad. Farfalle *(bows),* gnocchi *and shells would all be suitable alternatives.*

167 PASTA SALAD

Preparation time:
15 minutes, plus cooling

Cooking time:
10 minutes

Serves 4

Calories:
290 per portion

YOU WILL NEED:
100 g/4 oz shell or small shapes of pasta
about 300 ml/½ pint chicken stock
4 sticks celery, halved lengthwise and cut into strips
4 large tomatoes, quartered
1 garlic clove, peeled and crushed
1 tablespoon chopped fresh basil
100 g/4 oz Mozzarella cheese, grated
Lemon vinaigrette (see recipe 227), to serve

Cook the pasta in the boiling stock for about 10 minutes until just tender. Drain and leave to cool.

Mix the celery, pepper, tomatoes, garlic, pasta and basil together.

Sprinkle with the grated cheese. Serve a Lemon vinaigrette separately.

168 HERBED CHICKEN PASTA

Preparation time:
10 minutes, plus cooling

Cooking time:
20 minutes

Serves 4

Calories:
241 per portion

YOU WILL NEED:
100 g/4 oz shell pasta or macaroni
1 teaspoon chopped fresh oregano or ½ teaspoon dried oregano
1 teaspoon chopped fresh rosemary or ½ teaspoon dried rosemary
350 g/12 oz cooked chicken meat
100 g/4 oz mushrooms, chopped
1 tablespoon olive oil
1 teaspoon ground coriander
salt and pepper

Put the pasta into boiling, salted water with the herbs and cook for about 10 minutes until tender but still firm.

Cut the chicken meat into bite-sized pieces.

Add the chicken and mushrooms to the pasta and cook for a further 10 minutes. Drain if necessary. Set aside to cool.

Just before serving, add the olive oil and coriander and salt and pepper to taste.

COOK'S TIP

If this salad is to be part of a buffet, it would be more convenient to mix the dressing into it. Try another dressing for variety – the Green herb dressing (recipe 236) or the Tomato juice dressing (recipe 238) would be tasty alternatives.

COOK'S TIP

This makes an excellent main course salad, needing just a simple green salad to turn it into a satisfying meal.

169 LENTIL AND TOMATO SALAD

Preparation time:
15 minutes, plus soaking

Cooking time:
30-40 minutes

Serves 6

Calories:
259 per portion

YOU WILL NEED:
225 g/8 oz lentils, soaked for 1 hour
salt and pepper
6 tablespoons Tomato and garlic dressing (see Cook's Tip)
4 spring onions, chopped
4 tomatoes, skinned and chopped
2 celery sticks, sliced
1 tablespoon chopped parsley

Drain the lentils, place in a pan and cover with cold water. Add a little salt and simmer gently for 30-40 minutes until softened. Drain well and mix with the dressing while still warm. Leave to cool.

Add the remaining ingredients, seasoning with salt and pepper to taste. Mix together thoroughly.

Transfer to a salad bowl to serve.

COOK'S TIP

For Tomato and garlic dressing, mix well together 300 ml/½ pint tomato juice, 1 tablespoon lemon juice, 1 crushed garlic clove, 2 tablespoons chopped chives, 2 tablespoons olive oil and salt and pepper to taste.

170 CHICKEN RISOTTO

Preparation time:
5 minutes

Cooking time:
20 minutes

Serves 4

Calories:
263 per portion

YOU WILL NEED:
100 g/4 oz long-grain rice
500 ml/18 fl oz chicken stock
350 g/12 oz cooked chicken meat
1 dessertspoon chopped fresh tarragon or 1 teaspoon dried tarragon
salt and pepper
1 tablespoon tarragon vinegar
1 tablespoon olive oil

Put the rice in a saucepan and cover with the stock, reserving a little. Cover the pan and cook briskly, adding more stock if necessary.

Cut the chicken into bite-sized pieces.

Remove the rice from the heat when nearly cooked, after about 12 minutes. Stir in the tarragon and chicken.

Add more stock if the mixture is too dry and return to the heat for about 5 minutes until the chicken is hot. Add salt and pepper to taste. All the stock should be absorbed, if not, drain.

Set the risotto aside to cool. Just before serving, add the tarragon vinegar and olive oil to the risotto and mix well.

COOK'S TIP

This risotto makes a good hot dish: serve it while still hot from cooking, and without adding the tarragon vinegar and olive oil.

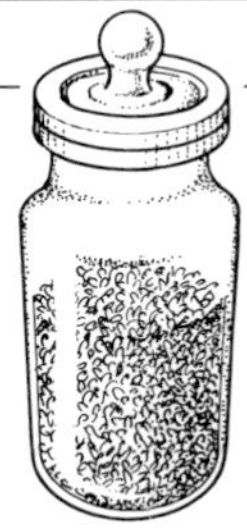

171 Brown Rice Salad

Preparation time:
10 minutes, plus cooling

Cooking time:
40-45 minutes

Serves 6

Calories:
319 per portion

YOU WILL NEED:
225 g/8 oz brown rice
salt
3 spring onions, finely chopped
1 red pepper, cored, seeded and chopped
50 g/2 oz raisins
50 g/2 oz cashew nuts, roasted and chopped
2 tablespoons chopped parsley (optional)
6 tablespoons Soy sauce dressing (see recipe 231)

Cook the rice in boiling salted water for 40-45 minutes until tender. Rinse, drain well and cool.

Place in a bowl and add the remaining ingredients. Toss thoroughly before serving.

COOK'S TIP

Brown rice is the natural rice grain before it has been processed. It needs to be cooked for a longer time than white rice, and in more water.

172 Prawn and Rice Salad

Preparation time:
10 minutes, plus cooling

Cooking time:
about 12 minutes

Serves 4

Calories:
241 per portion

YOU WILL NEED:
100 g/4 oz long-grain rice
fish stock (optional: see method)
lettuce leaves
1 cucumber, peeled and sliced
4 tomatoes, skinned and quartered
450 g/1 lb peeled prawns
grated rind and juice of 1 lemon
pinch of paprika or cayenne

Cook the rice in a saucepan of boiling fish stock, or salted water, for about 12 minutes until just tender.

Drain and leave to cool.

Place the lettuce in a salad bowl and add the cucumber slices and quartered tomatoes.

Mix the prawns and cold rice together. Stir in the lemon rind and paprika or cayenne.

Spoon into the centre of the bowl and sprinkle over the lemon juice.

COOK'S TIP

For a hotter flavoured salad, use Tabasco sauce instead of the paprika or cayenne and lemon juice. Add 50 g/2 oz cooked peas to the salad.

173 GREEN RICE

Preparation time:
10 minutes, plus cooling

Cooking time:
15 minutes

Serves 4

Calories:
194 per portion

YOU WILL NEED:
100 g/4 oz long-grain rice
salt and pepper
3 tablespoons olive oil
2 teaspoons white wine vinegar
squeeze of lemon juice
2 tablespoons chopped parsley
2 tablespoons chopped chives
1 tablespoon chopped dill
1 tablespoon chopped tarragon

Cook the rice in a saucepan of boiling salted water until tender; drain well. While the rice is still hot, stir in salt and pepper to taste, the olive oil, vinegar, and lemon juice. When the rice has cooled, stir in the chopped herbs.

COOK'S TIP

Serve this rice salad with cold fish dishes, cold meat and hard-boiled eggs, the flavours of all of which will be enhanced by the fresh herbs in the rice.

174 BROWN RICE AND HAZELNUT SALAD

Preparation time:
20 minutes

Cooking time:
30-40 minutes

Serves 6

Calories:
321 per portion

YOU WILL NEED:
175 g/6 oz brown rice
salt
75 g/3 oz hazelnuts, chopped and toasted
1 red pepper, cored, seeded and diced
6 spring onions, finely sliced
3 celery sticks, chopped
50 g/2 oz button mushrooms, sliced
6 tablespoons French dressing (see recipe 233)
3 tablespoons chopped parsley

Cook the rice in boiling salted water for 30-40 minutes, until tender. Rinse and drain well.

Place in a bowl with the remaining ingredients and toss thoroughly. Transfer to a shallow dish to serve.

COOK'S TIP

This is a good salad for vegetarians and wholefood addicts, being high in fibre, protein, iron, minerals and vitamins.

175 BUCKWHEAT AND CORN SALAD

Preparation time:
15 minutes

Cooking time:
about 15 minutes

Serves 4

Calories:
241 per portion

YOU WILL NEED:
75 g/3 oz toasted buckwheat (see Cook's Tip)
salt
4 tablespoons Ginger dressing (see recipe 234)
1 x 198 g/7 oz can sweetcorn, drained
1 green pepper, cored, seeded and chopped
3 tomatoes, skinned and chopped
2 tablespoons chopped parsley
25 g/1 oz toasted sunflower seeds

Place the buckwheat in a pan of boiling salted water, cover and simmer gently for 15 minutes. Drain thoroughly and place in a bowl with the dressing.

Add the remaining ingredients and toss thoroughly.

Transfer to a shallow dish to serve.

COOK'S TIP

Toasted buckwheat, called 'kasha' is available from health food stores. Buckwheat, the seed of a herbaceous plant, is rich in protein and iron.

176 WHOLEWHEAT SALAD

Preparation time:
15 minutes, plus cooling

Cooking time:
1-1½ hours

Serves 4

Calories:
398 per portion

YOU WILL NEED:
225 g/8 oz wheat, soaked overnight
salt
6 tablespoons Shoyu dressing (see recipe 234)
1 red pepper, cored, seeded and chopped
50 g/2 oz raisins
2 celery sticks, diced
2 tablespoons chopped parsley

Drain the wheat thoroughly. Place in a pan, cover with lightly salted water, bring to the boil and simmer for 1-1½ hours; drain well. Mix with the dressing while still warm, then leave to cool.

Add the remaining ingredients, toss well, then transfer to a shallow dish to serve.

COOK'S TIP

Using wholewheat in this salad greatly increases its dietary fibre content, since the grain retains the wheat germ and bran.

MAINLY FRUIT

There is more to a fruit salad than a pleasant dessert. As this chapter shows, fruit can be served at the beginning of a meal, too, in many unusual guises. Fruits also combine well with vegetables to make salads guaranteed to enhance the simplest meat dish, while fruit and cold meats such as ham form the basis of many salads.

177 HONEYDEW MELON SALAD

Preparation time:
15-20 minutes, plus chilling

Serves 4

Calories:
129 per portion

YOU WILL NEED:
1 honeydew melon
1 large fresh pineapple
4 tablespoons Cointreau or Curaçao
fresh cherries, to decorate

Slice the melon in half lengthways, scoop out and discard the seeds. Scoop out the flesh in large pieces and reserve. Using scissors or a very sharp knife serrate the edge of one of the melon halves to give a decorative edge.

Peel and core the pineapple and dice into chunks. Pile these and the melon pieces into the decorated melon half. Sprinkle over the liqueur and decorate with the washed and stoned cherries. Chill before serving.

COOK'S TIP

It is easier to core the pineapple if it is first cut into 1 cm/½ inch thick slices. A ripe pineapple has golden, not green, skin. It will also have a sweet aroma.

178 MELON SALAD

Preparation time:
10 minutes

Serves 4

Calories:
90 per portion

YOU WILL NEED:
2 ripe honeydew or Ogen melons, halved, seeded and peeled
1 small red pepper, cored, seeded and sliced
2 tablespoons lemon juice
1 tablespoon sunflower oil
1 teaspoon ground ginger
fresh salad vegetables, to garnish

Cut the melon flesh into 2 cm/¾ inch cubes and put them into a mixing bowl with the sliced red pepper. Combine the lemon juice with the oil and pour over the melon.

Sprinkle the salad with the ginger and fork through lightly to coat all the melon with dressing. Serve on individual salad plates with a garnish of fresh salad vegetables.

COOK'S TIP

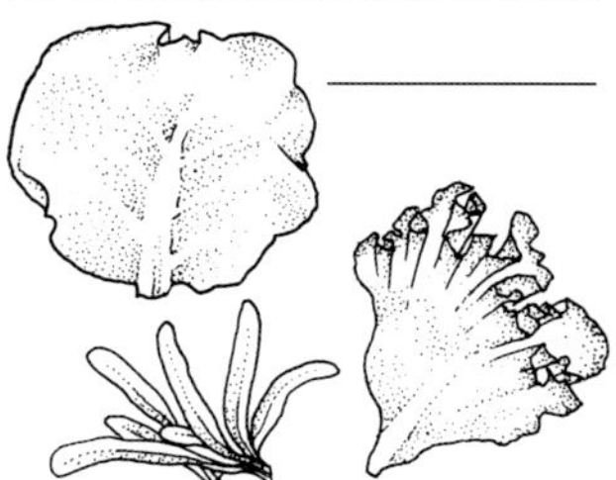

Different types of lettuce and cucumber can be used to garnish this delicately flavoured side salad. It makes a refreshing accompaniment to cold chicken or duck.

179 STUFFED MELONS

Preparation time:
30 minutes, plus chilling

Serves 8

Calories:
140 per portion

YOU WILL NEED:
2 Charentais, Ogen or small honeydew melons
2 nectarines, skinned, stoned and chopped
225 g/8 oz raspberries, hulled
2 kiwi fruit, peeled and chopped
100 g/4 oz seedless white grapes, halved
75 g/3 oz icing sugar
5 tablespoons Kirsch

Cut a tiny slice off the bottom of the melons so that they stand up. Then cut a slice off the top about 2.5 cm/1 inch down, so that the melon seeds and flesh can be scooped out easily without having too big a 'lid'. Scoop out the seeds and discard, then scoop out all the flesh and chop into small pieces.

Put the chopped melon into a bowl, add the nectarines, raspberries, kiwi fruit and grapes, then sprinkle with the sugar and Kirsch. Chill for 2 hours.

Pile the fruits back into the melon cases, distributing the juices evenly, and put the 'lids' back on (any fruit that will not fit into the melons can be kept to serve at another meal).

COOK'S TIP

If you seal the 'lids' with strong sticky tape and then wrap the melons tightly in cling wrap or foil, they can be packed in a cold box for a picnic.

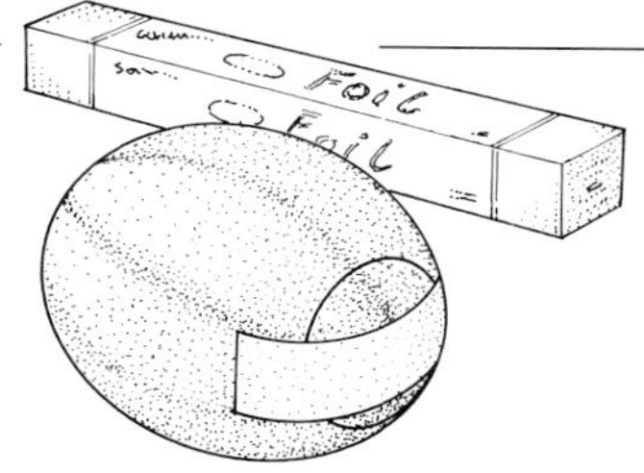

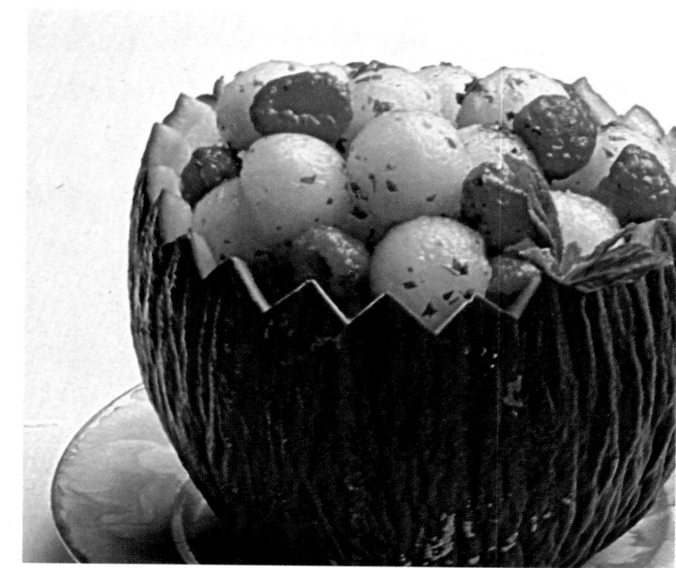

180 MELON WITH RASPBERRIES AND MINT

Preparation time:
15 minutes

Serves 4

Calories:
76 per portion

YOU WILL NEED:
1 honeydew melon
225 g/8 oz raspberries, hulled
2 tablespoons caster sugar
1 tablespoon chopped fresh mint

Cut a slice off the top of the melon, scoop out the seeds and discard. Cut out the flesh with a sharp-edged spoon and cut it into cubes or balls. Mix the raspberries lightly in a bowl with the melon cubes or balls. Mix the sugar and mint together in a cup. Tip them into the fruit and fold in carefully. Return the fruit to the melon shell to serve, or put it in a glass bowl.

COOK'S TIP

This salad should be served soon after it is prepared, otherwise the fruit will become soft and less appetizing.

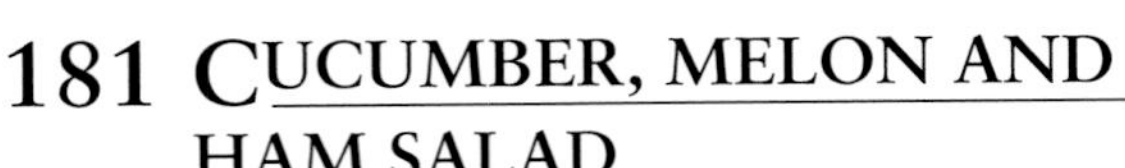

181 CUCUMBER, MELON AND HAM SALAD

Preparation time:
25 minutes

Serves 4

Calories:
189 per portion

YOU WILL NEED:
1 Ogen or small honeydew melon
1 slice cooked ham, about 225 g/8 oz
4 tomatoes, quartered
75 g/3 oz black grapes, halved and seeded
¼ cucumber, very thinly sliced
fresh mint sprigs, for garnish
FOR THE DRESSING
4 tablespoons soured cream
2 tablespoons chopped spring onions
1 teaspoon chopped fresh mint
salt and pepper

Slice the melon in half, scoop out the seeds and discard. Remove the flesh with a melon baller or cut into bite-sized cubes. Reserve the melon shells for serving if wished.

Cut the ham into thin julienne strips. Place in a bowl with the melon, tomatoes, grapes and cucumber, tossing gently to mix.

Mix the soured cream with the spring onion, mint and salt and pepper to taste. Combine the salad ingredients with the dressing, tossing gently to mix.

Spoon into a serving bowl or return to the melon shells to serve. Garnish with a few sprigs of mint before serving.

COOK'S TIP

The dressing can be made in advance and stored in the refrigerator for up to 3 days. Stir well to blend before using.

182 GRAPEFRUIT AND AVOCADO SALAD

Preparation time:
15-20 minutes

Serves 6

Calories:
337 per portion

YOU WILL NEED:
3 ripe, firm avocados
1 large cooked potato, diced
1 pink grapefruit, peeled and segmented
1 teaspoon crushed peppercorns or fresh chervil sprig to garnish
FOR THE DRESSING
3 tablespoons olive oil
1 tablespoon walnut oil
1 small garlic clove, crushed
2 tablespoons lemon juice or white wine vinegar
salt and pepper

Peel the avocados, remove the stones, and cut into small chunks. Place in a salad bowl with the diced potato and grapefruit segments and mix gently.

Combine all the dressing ingredients, whisk with a fork to blend thoroughly, and pour over the salad. Fork gently through, sprinkle with the crushed peppercorns or garnish with chervil and serve immediately.

COOK'S TIP

This attractive salad, with its unusual combination of flavours and textures, should be prepared just before serving. It goes especially well with spiced beef or ham.

183 MELON, TOMATO AND GRAPE SHELLS

Preparation time:
20 minutes

Serves 4

Calories:
119 per portion

YOU WILL NEED:
2 small Ogen melons
4 tomatoes, skinned, quartered, and seeded
175 g/6 oz black grapes, halved and seeded
4 tablespoons Mint and honey dressing (see recipe 232)
1 tablespoon sesame seeds, roasted (see recipe 109)
4 mint sprigs, to garnish

Cut the melons in half and discard the seeds. Scoop the flesh into balls, using a melon baller, or cut into cubes; reserve the shells. Place the melon in a bowl with the tomatoes and grapes. Pour over the dressing.

Toss well, then spoon the mixture into the melon shells. Sprinkle with the roasted sesame seeds and garnish with the mint sprigs.

COOK'S TIP

Melon shells make decorative containers for other salad mixtures to be served as starters for a summer lunch or dinner party.

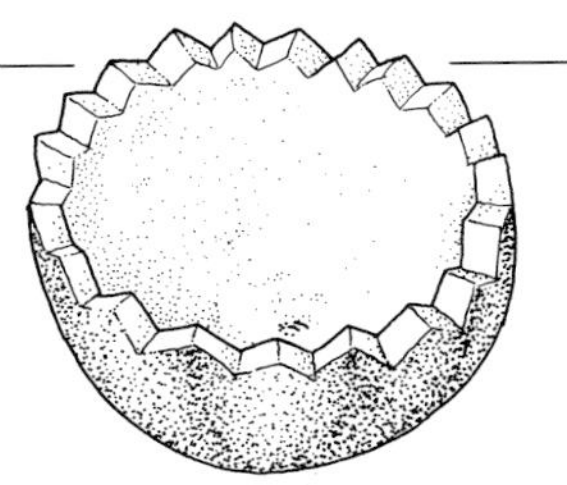

184 GRAPEFRUIT SALAD

Preparation time:
20 minutes

Serves 6

Calories:
163 per portion

YOU WILL NEED:
3 grapefruit, peeled and segmented
10-12 heads corn salad or 1 bunch watercress
½ small cos lettuce
75 g/3 oz halved almonds, blanched and toasted
FOR THE DRESSING
3 tablespoons olive oil
2 shallots, finely chopped
1 tablespoon lemon juice
1 teaspoon clear honey
salt and pepper

Toss together the grapefruit and corn salad or watercress. Mix together the ingredients for the dressing, pour over the salad and toss well.

Tear the cos lettuce leaves into small pieces and use to line a serving dish.

Just before serving, stir the almonds into the grapefruit salad and spoon it carefully on to the bed of lettuce.

COOK'S TIP

Pink grapefruit are the ideal choice for this tangy salad, which makes a particularly good accompaniment to grilled poultry and fish.

185 BEETROOT AND ORANGE SALAD

Preparation time:
15 minutes, plus chilling

Serves 4

Calories:
207 per portion

YOU WILL NEED:
2 large oranges
4 tablespoons French dressing (see recipe 233)
1 garlic clove, finely sliced (optional)
450 g/1 lb cooked beetroot, sliced
watercress or mint sprigs, to garnish

Grate the rind from one of the oranges and mix with the dressing. Add the garlic, if using. Peel and thinly slice both oranges, removing all pith.

Arrange the orange and beetroot slices in alternate layers in a serving dish. Pour the dressing over the top and garnish with watercress or mint sprigs. Chill before serving.

COOK'S TIP

This colourful salad looks most attractive when served in a shallow circular dish to emphasize the shape of the sliced oranges and beetroot.

186 LEEK, TOMATO AND ORANGE SALAD

Preparation time:
15 minutes

Serves 4

Calories:
63 per portion

YOU WILL NEED:
4 tomatoes, sliced
2 oranges, sliced
4 small leeks, finely sliced, using the white part only
lemon juice

Arrange the tomato and orange slices round the edge of a serving dish. Put the leeks in the centre of the dish. Sprinkle the leeks with a little lemon juice. Serve with Lemon vinaigrette (see recipe 227).

COOK'S TIP

Cooks with vegetable gardens can use the young leeks taken from the unthinned seedlings left over after planting for salads such as this one.

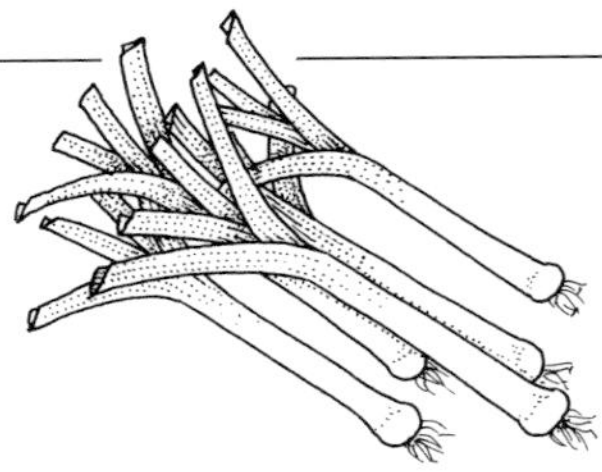

187 CELERY, APPLE AND SESAME SALAD

Preparation time:
10 minutes

Serves 6

Calories:
127 per portion

YOU WILL NEED:
1 head celery, thinly sliced
4 red-skinned dessert apples, cored and thinly sliced
4 tablespoons Vinaigrette dressing (see recipe 225)
1 tablespoon sesame seeds, roasted (see recipe 109)

Place the celery and apple slices in a salad bowl. Pour in the dressing and toss well.

Just before serving, mix in the sesame seeds.

188 APPLE AND CABBAGE SLAW

Preparation time:
15 minutes

Serves 6

Calories:
189 per portion

YOU WILL NEED:
1 head white cabbage
4 red apples
1 tablespoon lemon juice
1 small green pepper, cored, seeded and diced
1 onion, finely sliced
6 tablespoons French dressing (see recipe 233)
25 g/1 oz Edam cheese, grated

Shred the cabbage finely and place in a large bowl. Remove the cores from the apples and slice apples thinly, sprinkling with lemon juice to prevent them from going brown. Add to the bowl with the diced green pepper, onion and dressing. Toss lightly and sprinkle with the grated cheese.

COOK'S TIP

Keep sesame seeds in an air-tight jar, roasting them as required (see recipe 109). Like other nuts and seeds, they are rich in B vitamins, minerals and proteins.

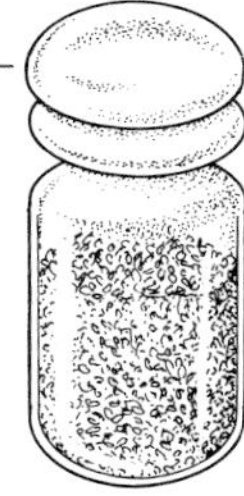

COOK'S TIP

Instead of the French dressing, you could use a soured cream or yogurt dressing equally successfully with this type of salad.

189 APPLEMINT BOWL

Preparation time:
15 minutes

Serves 4

Calories:
175 per portion

YOU WILL NEED:
3 dessert apples, cored and thinly sliced
75 g/3 oz raw peanuts
4 celery sticks, thinly sliced
fresh mint and marjoram sprigs, to garnish
FOR THE DRESSING
1 teaspoon grated lemon rind
2 tablespoons lemon juice
2 tablespoons chopped fresh mint
1 tablespoon chopped marjoram
4 tablespoons natural yogurt

Mix the dressing until it is smooth, and have it ready before you slice the apples.

Toss together the apples, peanuts and celery and stir in the dressing. Toss to coat the fruit thoroughly. Garnish with the chopped mint and marjoram.

COOK'S TIP

Try using the decorative apple mint with its faint taste of sage if serving this salad with pork. If fresh marjoram is not available, you can substitute parsley.

190 APPLE TREE SALAD

Preparation time:
20 minutes

Serves 6

Calories:
115 per portion

YOU WILL NEED:
2 dessert apples, cored and thinly sliced
2 teaspoons lemon juice
225 g/8 oz button mushrooms, thinly sliced
225 g/8 oz black grapes, halved and seeded
2 carrots, scraped and grated
2 tablespoons roasted sesame seeds (see recipe 109)
FOR THE DRESSING
2 tablespoons olive oil
1 tablespoon cloudy apple juice
2 tablespoons soured cream
salt and pepper

Mix the dressing ingredients until they are well blended.

Toss the apples in the lemon juice. Reserve a few apple and mushroom slices for garnish. Mix together the remaining apple and mushroom slices, the grapes, carrots and sesame seeds.

Pour on the dressing and mix well. Garnish the salad with the reserved apple and mushroom slices.

COOK'S TIP

If you have an electric juice extractor, cloudy apple juice can be produced in seconds. Otherwise buy it from health food stores.

191 MOROCCAN ORANGE SALAD

Preparation time:
20 minutes, plus chilling

Serves 4

Calories:
177 per portion

YOU WILL NEED:
4 large or 6 medium oranges
50 g/2 oz dates, roughly chopped
25 g/1 oz flaked almonds
2 tablespoons caster sugar
juice of 2 lemons
ground cinnamon, to decorate

Peel and slice the oranges, discarding the pith. Place in a serving dish with the dates and almonds.

Mix together the sugar and lemon juice and pour over the fruit mixture. Chill for at least 2 hours before serving.

Sprinkle with cinnamon to taste.

COOK'S TIP

If liked, serve cream with this orange salad. Alternatively, the calorie-conscious might prefer fromage frais which combines well with oranges.

192 ORANGE AND CELERY SALAD

Preparation time:
15 minutes

Serves 4

Calories:
222 per portion

YOU WILL NEED:
4 oranges, peeled and segmented
1 head celery, finely sliced
1 mild onion, coarsely chopped
1 teaspoon coriander seeds, lightly crushed
celery leaves, to garnish
FOR THE DRESSING
2 tablespoons red wine vinegar or lemon juice
5 tablespoons olive oil
salt and pepper

Place the orange segments, celery and onion in a salad bowl. Fork through lightly to mix. Sprinkle with the coriander seeds.

Combine all the dressing ingredients and whisk together with a fork to blend thoroughly. Pour over the salad, toss gently and garnish with celery leaves.

COOK'S TIP

Wash the celery very thoroughly in cold water to remove any grit or soil. Large Spanish onions are a mild variety.

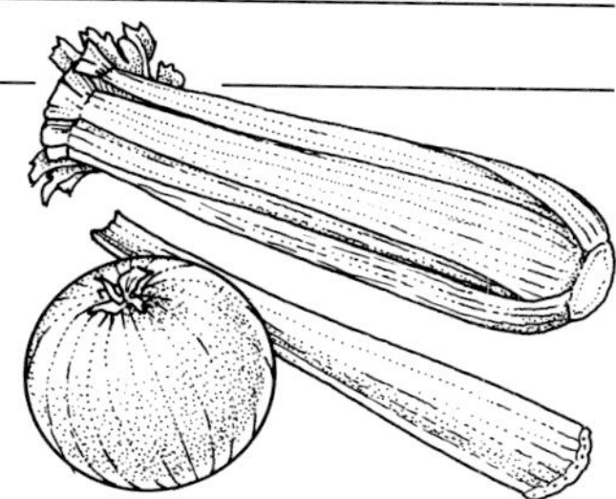

193 ORANGE AND DANDELION SALAD

Preparation time:
15 minutes

Serves 4

Calories:
64 per portion

YOU WILL NEED:
450 g/1 lb young dandelion leaves, curly endive or young spinach leaves
2 oranges, sliced and quartered
1 bunch watercress
50 g/2 oz spring onions, chopped

Shred the dandelion leaves, curly endive or spinach leaves and pile into a serving dish. Arrange the orange slices and watercress on top. Scatter over the chopped spring onions.

Serve with Orange vinaigrette (see recipe 227).

COOK'S TIP

Wash and dry the dandelion leaves carefully. Cut out the central core and the stalk of any that are past their prime.

194 ORANGE AND MINT SALAD

Preparation time:
10 minutes

Serves 4

Calories:
62 per portion

YOU WILL NEED:
4 large oranges
2 tablespoons finely chopped fresh mint
3 tablespoons lemon juice
4 tablespoons wine vinegar
caster sugar
salt and pepper
mint sprigs, to garnish

Remove all the peel and pith from the oranges and cut the flesh into thin slices. Place in a serving dish and sprinkle with the chopped mint. Mix the lemon juice with the vinegar, adding sugar to taste. Season with salt and pepper and pour over the orange slices. Garnish with mint sprigs.

COOK'S TIP

The sharpness of the dressing makes this a suitable salad to serve with a rich main course dish such as roast duck.

195 PEACH AND SOURED CREAM SALAD

Preparation time:
15 minutes, plus chilling

Serves 4

Calories:
62 per portion

YOU WILL NEED:
1 lettuce, shredded
4 firm peaches
2 teaspoons mild curry powder
2 teaspoons caster sugar
2 teaspoons lemon juice
4 tablespoons soured cream
1 garlic clove, very finely chopped

Arrange the shredded lettuce on 4 individual plates. Wash and stone the peaches, then slice into 1 cm/½ inch pieces

Mix together the curry powder, sugar, lemon juice, soured cream and garlic. Arrange the peaches on top of the lettuce and spoon over the soured cream dressing. Chill before serving.

196 FRESH FRUIT SALAD

Preparation time:
20 minutes

Serves 4

Calories:
122 per portion

YOU WILL NEED:
2 dessert apples, peeled and sliced
1 banana, sliced
juice of 1 lemon
3 oranges
1 grapefruit, peeled, sliced and halved
100 g/4 oz grapes, seeded
sifted icing sugar (optional)

Toss the apple and banana slices in the lemon juice to prevent discoloration. Peel and slice one of the oranges and squeeze the juice from the remaining two. Remove any pith and pips from the orange and grapefruit slices.

Add the orange, grapefruit and grapes to the apple and banana slices, and mix well. Add the orange juice and a little sugar to taste, if necessary.

COOK'S TIP

This salad makes an original starter or it can be served as an accompaniment to cold roast poultry. Replace the soured cream with yogurt for a less rich dressing.

COOK'S TIP

Serve this fresh fruit salad for breakfast if you are an early-riser and can prepare it in time!

197 RED FRUIT COMPOTE WITH RASPBERRY SAUCE

Preparation time:
25 minutes, plus chilling

Cooking time:
about 15 minutes

Serves 8

Calories:
184 per portion

YOU WILL NEED:
grated rind of 1 lemon
2.5 cm/1 inch piece cinnamon stick
2 cloves
275 g/10 oz caster sugar
600 ml/1 pint water
450 g/1 lb redcurrants and/or blackcurrants, stringed
450 g/1 lb strawberries, hulled and sliced
225 g/8 oz raspberries, hulled
1 teaspoon lemon juice
sifted icing sugar
1 tablespoon Cassis or Framboise liqueur

Put the lemon rind, cinnamon stick, cloves and sugar in a saucepan with the water and stir over a very gentle heat until the sugar is dissolved. Bring to the boil and boil for about 5 minutes until syrupy. Add the redcurrants and strawberries to the pan and poach gently for about 10 minutes. Strain, reserving the liquid and add some of the poaching liquid as necessary to achieve a smooth pouring consistency. Stir in the chosen liqueur.

Pour the sauce over the compote in a glass serving bowl and chill for 2-3 hours before serving.

COOK'S TIP

The choice of liqueur depends on whether you prefer to emphasize the flavours of the blackcurrants or the raspberries in the compote.

198 KIWI AND GINGER SALAD

Preparation time:
20 minutes

Serves 4

Calories:
114 per portion

YOU WILL NEED:
1 Ogen melon, halved and seeded
2 kiwi fruit, thinly sliced
250 g/9 oz green grapes, halved and seeded
15 g/½ oz stem ginger, thinly sliced
2 tablespoons ginger syrup (from the ginger)
4 tablespoons apple juice

Scoop the flesh from the melon halves with a melon baller, or cut into cubes, and place in a bowl with the kiwi fruit, grapes and ginger.

Mix the ginger syrup and apple juice together and pour over the fruit. Serve in individual dishes.

COOK'S TIP

Kiwi fruit can be frozen successfully for several months, so buy them when you see any bargains in your local shops or market.

199 WATERMELON WITH HONEY

Preparation time:
10 minutes, plus chilling

Serves 4

Calories:
78 per portion

YOU WILL NEED:
1 small watermelon
2 tablespoons clear honey
juice of ½ lemon
2 tablespoons dry sherry
25 g/1 oz flaked almonds, roasted

Scoop the flesh out of the watermelon, discarding the seeds, and cut into cubes.

Mix together the honey, lemon juice and sherry, then fold in the melon. Chill for 1 hour.

Spoon into glasses and sprinkle with the almonds to serve.

■ COOK'S TIP

Perfect for a heatwave! If you cannot find a suitably small watermelon, buy one of the large wedges often sold in supermarkets.

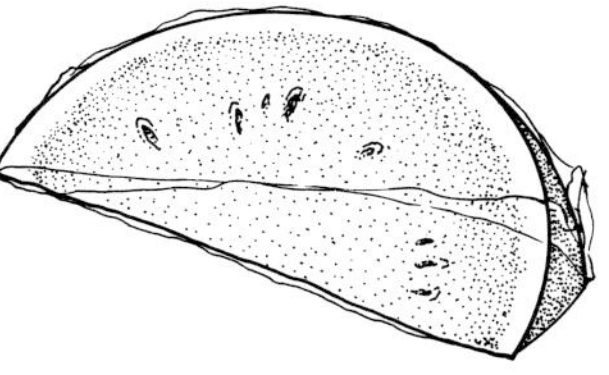

200 MIXED MELON SALAD

Preparation time:
15 minutes, plus chilling

Serves 4

Calories:
90 per portion

YOU WILL NEED:
1 small Ogen melon, peeled and cut into 2.5 cm/1 inch cubes
1 small honeydew melon, peeled and cut into 2.5 cm/1 inch cubes
1 slice watermelon, peeled and cut into 2.5 cm/1 inch cubes
juice of 2 limes
juice of 1 small orange
1-2 tablespoons caster sugar (optional)
½-1 tablespoon finely chopped fresh mint

Put the three types of melon into a serving bowl, pour over the citrus fruit juices and stir well to mix. Sweeten with a little sugar if liked. Stir in the chopped mint and chill for 1-2 hours before serving.

■ COOK'S TIP

When watermelon is out of season, 225 g/8 oz hulled raspberries can be used instead to give colour contrast. For extra-special occasions the melon flesh can be cut with a melon baller and the fruit salad served in the honeydew melon shell.

201 RED FRUIT SALAD

Preparation time:
30 minutes, plus chilling and overnight draining

Cooking time:
5 minutes

Serves 4

Calories:
227 per portion

YOU WILL NEED:
675 g/1½ lb raspberries, hulled
4 tablespoons clear honey
225 g/8 oz dessert cherries, stoned
225 g/8 oz blackcurrants, stringed
grated nutmeg, to decorate
FOR THE CURD CHEESE
2 teaspoons powdered gelatine
2 tablespoons hot water
350 g/12 oz cottage cheese, sieved
150 ml/¼ pint natural yogurt
4 tablespoons double cream

Dissolve the gelatine in the hot water in a small bowl over a pan of simmering water.

Beat together the cottage cheese, yogurt and cream, then stir in the dissolved gelatine. Spoon the mixture into 4 draining moulds or yogurt pots. To use yogurt pots, cover them with muslin and invert them to drain over a dish. Leave overnight.

Blend half the raspberries in a liquidizer, then sieve them. Stir the honey into the purée over a low heat. Stir in the remaining raspberries, the cherries and blackcurrants and simmer for 2-3 minutes. Cool, then chill in the refrigerator for at least 1 hour.

Turn out the curd cheese moulds and decorate them with a pinch of grated nutmeg. Serve them with the fruit salad as a substantial 'sauce'.

COOK'S TIP

You can freeze the fruit salad during the soft fruit season but the curd cheese moulds must be made the day before they are served.

202 GINGER FRUIT SALAD

Preparation time:
20 minutes

Serves 4

Calories:
120 per portion

YOU WILL NEED:
2 apples, cored but not peeled
2 apricots, peeled
1 orange, peeled and segmented
250 ml/8 fl oz bottle ginger ale
2 bananas
2 tablespoons lemon juice
50 g/2 oz green grapes, seeded

Dice the apples and apricots and mix together with the orange segments in a bowl. Pour over the ginger ale. Slice the bananas and mix with the lemon juice and grapes. Mix all the fruit and juices together and serve in individual glasses.

COOK'S TIP

If you would like to make this salad when fresh apricots are out-of-season, substitute the ready-to-eat dried ones.

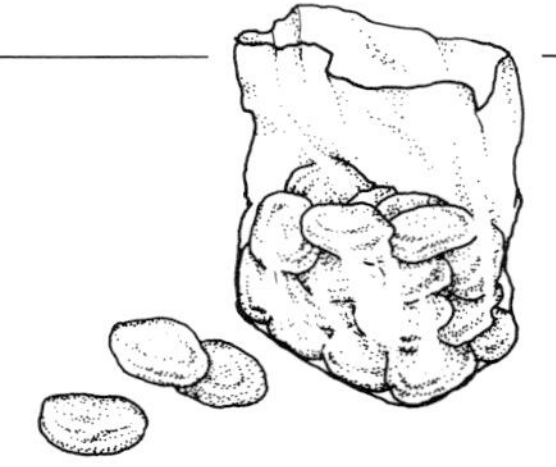

203 PEARS EN COMPOTE

Preparation time:
5 minutes, plus chilling

Cooking time:
about 10 minutes

Serves 4

Calories:
190 per portion

YOU WILL NEED:
1 x 575 g/1¼ lb can pear halves
300 ml/½ pint red wine
2 teaspoons ground cinnamon
50 g/2 oz dates, chopped

Drain the pears, reserving 150 ml/¼ pint of the juice. Place the pears, wine, reserved pear juice and cinnamon in a pan. Bring to the boil, then lower the heat, cover and simmer for 10 minutes.

Add the dates, remove from the heat and leave to cool. Serve chilled, with cream if liked.

COOK'S TIP

A teetotal version of this compote can be made using red grape juice, adding a little food colouring if wished.

204 RHUBARB COMPOTE

Preparation time:
5-7 minutes, plus cooling

Cooking time:
5-10 minutes

Serves 4

Calories:
30 per portion

YOU WILL NEED:
675 g/1½ lb rhubarb, cut into 2.5 cm/ 1 inch pieces
4 tablespoons caster sugar
young angelica leaves, to decorate (optional)
1 teaspoon chopped crystallized angelica

Just cover the bottom of a large, heavy-based saucepan with a little cold water. Add the rhubarb, sugar and fresh angelica. Bring to the boil, then lower the heat, cover the pan and simmer gently for 5-10 minutes until the rhubarb is tender, stirring once or twice.

Spoon the rhubarb into individual glasses and cool for 1-2 hours.

Decorate with angelica leaves, if using, and crystallized angelica just before serving with cream or natural yogurt.

COOK'S TIP

The compote can be served either at room temperature or chilled. It makes a refreshing dessert after a substantial main course.

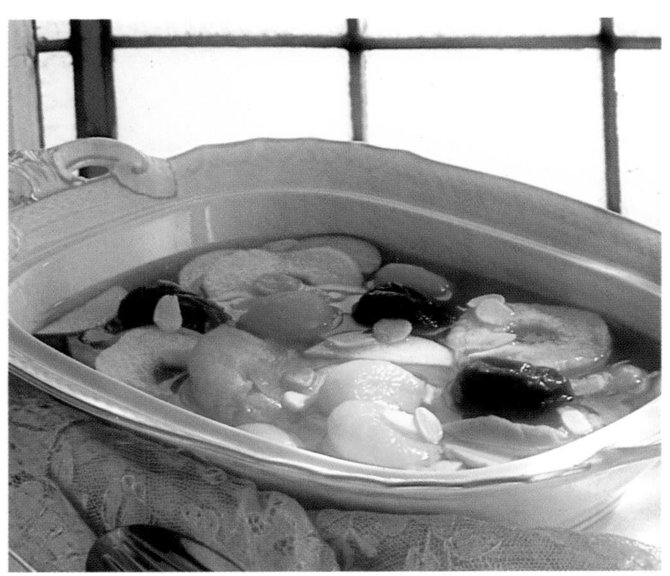

205 GINGERED FRUITS

Preparation time:
10 minutes, plus cooling and overnight soaking

Cooking time:
30 minutes

Serves 6

Calories:
258 per portion

YOU WILL NEED:
450 g/1 lb mixed dried fruits, soaked overnight in 600 ml/1 pint water
1 x 2·5 cm/1 inch piece fresh root ginger, peeled and halved
4 tablespoons ginger wine
2 teaspoons lemon juice
2 dessert apples, cored and thinly sliced
2 tablespoons blanched almonds, toasted
FOR THE SAUCE
250 ml/8 fl oz natural yogurt
2 pieces preserved ginger, finely chopped
1 tablespoon ginger syrup from the jar
1 teaspoon lemon juice

Put the dried fruit in a pan with the remaining soaking water, the pieces of ginger, ginger wine and lemon juice and bring slowly to the boil. Simmer for 25 minutes, or until the fruits are tender. Leave to cool.

Remove the pieces of ginger. Stir in the apple slices and, just before serving, the toasted almonds.

Mix together the yogurt, chopped ginger, syrup and lemon juice. Serve the fruits cold but not chilled, with the sauce separately.

COOK'S TIP

Combine many different types of dried fruit: apple rings, apricots, bananas, figs, peaches, pears and prunes. Add some dates to the pan, too.

206 SPICED MANGO SALAD

Preparation time:
20 minutes

Serves 4

Calories:
704 per portion

YOU WILL NEED:
1 curly endive, leaves separated
3 mangoes, peeled, stoned and thinly sliced
2 dessert apples, cored and chopped
2 teaspoons lemon juice
3 tablespoons pecan nuts
FOR THE DRESSING
1 egg
½ teaspoon Worcestershire sauce
1 tablespoon lemon juice
2 tablespoons natural yogurt
salt and pepper

Arrange the endive leaves to cover the base of a serving dish.

Whisk the egg together with all the other ingredients for the dressing. Toss the mango in the dressing. Arrange the mango slices in a wheel pattern over the endive and pour on any remaining dressing.

Toss the apple in the lemon juice and stir in the pecan nuts. Pile the apple and nuts in the centre.

COOK'S TIP

Choose mangoes when they feel slightly soft to the touch. They bruise quite easily so handle them gently.

207 DATE AND NUT SALAD

Preparation time:
10 minutes

Serves 4

Calories:
191 per portion

YOU WILL NEED:
175 g/6 oz dates, stoned and halved
3 crisp dessert apples, cored and sliced
50 g/2 oz walnut pieces
3 tablespoons lemon juice
150 ml/¼ pint natural yogurt
salt

Put the dates, apples and walnuts in a serving bowl. Mix together the lemon juice and yogurt and add salt to taste. Pour over the salad in the serving bowl and toss well until the ingredients are evenly coated.

COOK'S TIP

This salad mixture is ideal for filling into a lidded plastic container as part of a healthy packed lunch.

208 FRUIT AND NUT SALAD

Preparation time:
20 minutes, plus cooling

Cooking time:
about 15 minutes

Serves 6

Calories:
828 per portion

YOU WILL NEED:
225 g/8 oz shelled broad beans
1 dessert apple, cored and thinly sliced
2 dessert pears, peeled, cored and thinly sliced
1 tablespoon water
1 tablespoon lemon juice
1 bunch watercress
2 tablespoons macadamia nuts
2 tablespoons walnut halves
salad leaves, to serve
1 orange, peeled and segmented
FOR THE DRESSING
150 ml/¼ pint natural yogurt
2 tablespoons orange juice
1 tablespoon clear honey
2 tablespoons chopped mint
1 spring onion, thinly sliced
salt and pepper

Cook the beans in boiling, salted water for about 15 minutes until they are just tender. Drain, plunge into cold water, then drain again and cool. Meanwhile mix the dressing.

Toss the apple and pear slices in the water and lemon juice as they are cut, then drain them. Mix together the beans, apple and pear slices and watercress sprigs. Pour on the dressing and toss so that the salad is well coated. Stir in the macadamia nuts.

Arrange in a serving dish lined with salad leaves, and garnish with the orange segments.

COOK'S TIP

Macadamia nuts have an almost buttery mixture and are creamy coloured. They are considered a delicacy and are comparatively expensive.

209 BAKED FRUIT SALAD

Preparation time:
10 minutes

Cooking time:
about 20 minutes

Oven temperature:
200 C/400 F/Gas 6

Serves 4

Calories:
84 per portion

YOU WILL NEED:
1 grapefruit
2 oranges
1 dessert apple, sliced – Cox's Orange Pippin preferably
8 dried apricot halves
300 ml/½ pint unsweetened orange juice

Slice the grapefruit and oranges, leaving on the peel. Place the grapefruit, orange and apple slices in a casserole with the apricots. Use the ends of the oranges and grapefruit to cover the top.

Pour in the orange juice and cover. Bake in a preheated oven for about 20 minutes until all the fruit is soft. Serve hot or cold.

COOK'S TIP

Choose unblemished fruit as the peel is not removed. Scrub the grapefruit and oranges thoroughly before slicing to remove the coating of preservative.

210 PEACHES IN ORANGE JUICE

Preparation time:
5 minutes

Cooking time:
about 20 minutes

Oven temperature:
180 C/350 F/Gas 4

Serves 4

Calories:
72 per portion

YOU WILL NEED:
4 x 175 g/6 oz ripe peaches, skinned
250 ml/8 fl oz unsweetened orange juice

Cut the peaches in half and remove the stones. Place in a soufflé dish and pour the orange juice over. Cook in a preheated oven for 20 minutes or until tender.

COOK'S TIP

The peaches can be served immediately or be left to cool. The smaller and paler fruits tend to have the best flavour.

211 HOT FRUIT SALAD

Preparation time:
5 minutes, plus overnight soaking

Cooking time:
10-15 minutes

Serves 6

Calories:
229 per portion

YOU WILL NEED:
175 g/6 oz dried apricots
100 g/4 oz dried prunes
100 g/4 oz dried figs
100 g/4 oz dried apples
600 ml/1 pint apple juice
2 tablespoons Calvados or brandy
25 g/1 oz walnuts, coarsely chopped

Place the dried fruits in a bowl with the apple juice and leave to soak overnight.

Transfer to a saucepan and simmer for 10-15 minutes. Turn into a glass bowl and pour over the Calvados or brandy. Sprinkle with the walnuts. Serve immediately with natural yogurt.

COOK'S TIP

This fruit salad is equally good if made in advance and served cold. The alcohol can be omitted if preferred.

212 SET-ALIGHT SALAD

Preparation time:
20 minutes

Cooking time:
about 10 minutes

Serves 6

Calories:
66 per portion

YOU WILL NEED:
150 ml/¼ pint red grape juice
2 tablespoons water
1 tablespoon lemon juice
2 bay leaves
450 g/1 lb redcurrants, stringed
225 g/8 oz gooseberries, topped and tailed
225 g/8 oz raspberries, hulled
2 tablespoons brandy

To make the syrup, bring the grape juice, water, lemon juice and bay leaves to the boil in a large pan and simmer for 3 minutes.

Add the redcurrants and gooseberries and bring to the boil in the syrup. Simmer for 3-4 minutes.

Add the raspberries and just return to the boil. Transfer the fruit and syrup to a serving dish, removing the bay leaves, if preferred.

Pour the brandy into a warmed ladle and set light to it. Pour the flaming brandy on to the fruit. Serve at once.

COOK'S TIP

You can prepare the syrup in advance, then quickly reheat it when you have prepared all the fruit and are ready to serve the salad.

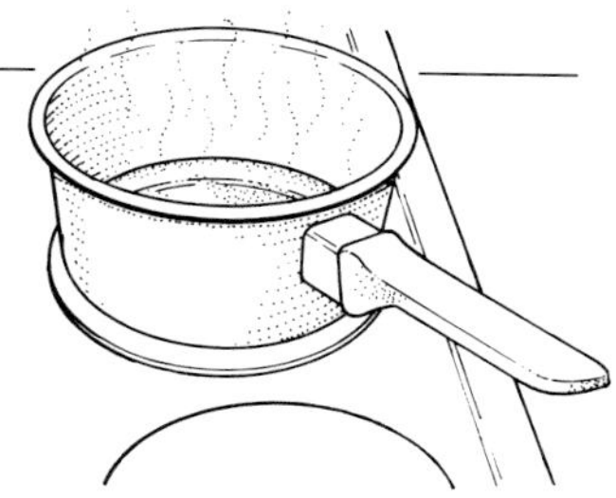

SAUCES, DIPS & DRESSINGS

Dressings, simple or complex, rich or light on calories; classic sauces and egg-rich mayonnaises; and mouth-watering dips make up this chapter.

213 YOGURT SAUCE WITH HERBS

Preparation time:
12 minutes, plus chilling

Serves 4

Calories:
21 per portion

YOU WILL NEED:
1 large garlic clove, crushed
pinch of salt
150 ml/¼ pint natural yogurt
freshly ground black pepper
½ tablespoon each chopped fresh tarragon, chervil, chives and parsley
½ tablespoon chopped fresh herbs, to garnish

Put the garlic into a bowl, add salt and mash together with a fork, to make a paste. Gradually beat in the yogurt.

Taste and adjust the seasoning, then stir in the herbs, cover and chill in the refrigerator for at least 1 hour before serving, sprinkling the chopped garnish herbs over the sauce at the last minute.

214 HERB REMOULADE

Preparation time:
15 minutes

Serves 4

Calories:
737 per portion

YOU WILL NEED:
2 hard-boiled egg yolks
2 raw eggs
salt and pepper
1 tablespoon Dijon mustard
300 ml/½ pint olive oil
2 tablespoons white wine vinegar
1 tablespoon tarragon vinegar
1 tablespoon dill vinegar
6 tablespoons sour cream or natural yogurt
4-5 tablespoons chopped mixed herbs: chervil, dill, chives, cress and parsley

Mash the hard-boiled egg yolks in a bowl with a fork, and beat in the raw yolks to make a paste. Add a pinch of salt, some black pepper and the mustard, and beat until smooth. Start adding the oil drop by drop, beating all the time. Thin with a teaspoon of the vinegar if it gets too thick. Continue to beat until all the oil is used up, then add the remaining vinegars. (If you have no tarragon or dill vinegar, simple substitute white wine vinegar.) When the sauce is smooth, stir in the sour cream (or yogurt), and the chopped herbs.

COOK'S TIP

Try mixing this sauce with grated celeriac, turnip or mooli for a crunchy, creamy salad.

COOK'S TIP

This subtle rémoulade (omitting the chopped capers and gherkins of the basic recipe), may be served with crudités, vegetable salads, hard-boiled eggs, and cold meats, such as roast beef salads.

215 EGG AND HERB SAUCE

Preparation time:
10 minutes

Serves 4

Calories:
121 per portion

YOU WILL NEED:
2 hard-boiled egg yolks
2 tablespoons thick cream
2 tablespoons olive oil
2 teaspoons white wine vinegar
salt and pepper
1 tablespoon chopped chives
1 tablespoon chopped dill
1 tablespoon chopped tarragon

Mash the egg yolks to a paste with the cream. Add the oil very gradually, stirring all the time, then the vinegar. Add salt and pepper to taste, then the chopped herbs. Serve with salads of all sorts.

COOK'S TIP

Although only the egg yolks are used in this sauce, the whites need not be wasted: chop them up and sprinkle them over the salad with which the sauce is served.

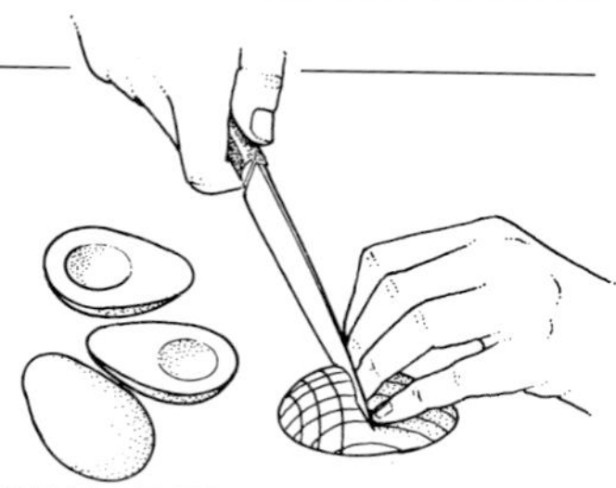

216 YOGURT AND MINT SAUCE

Preparation time:
15 minutes

Serves 4

Calories:
45 per portion

YOU WILL NEED:
300 ml/½ pint natural yogurt
1 cucumber
1-2 garlic cloves
salt and pepper
24 mint leaves

Beat the yogurt in a bowl until smooth. Peel the cucumber and grate it coarsely. Squeeze out the excess moisture from the cucumber between the hands. Peel and crush the garlic. Purée the yogurt, cucumber and garlic in a blender with salt and pepper and the mint leaves. Chill before serving.

COOK'S TIP

This makes a generous amount to serve with hot or cold roast or grilled lamb or poured over a dish of hot boiled new potatoes. It is also good used as a dressing on salads of crisp vegetables and fruit, like celery, apple and fennel.

217 DILL SAUCE

Preparation time:
5 minutes

Cooking time:
10-12 minutes

Serves 4:

Calories:
141 per portion

YOU WILL NEED:
25 g/1 oz butter
1 tablespoon flour
300 ml/½ pint beef stock or chicken stock
150 ml/¼ pint thin cream
1 teaspoon Dijon mustard
salt and pepper
3 tablespoons chopped dill

Melt the butter in a pan, stir in the flour and cook for 1-2 minutes, stirring. Heat the stock with the cream and pour on; blend and simmer gently for about 4 minutes. Stir in the mustard and add salt and pepper to taste. Add the chopped dill just before serving.

COOK'S TIP

Serve this sauce cold with skinned tomatoes and with salads, especially green leaf salads, potato and cucumber salads.

218 GARLIC AND HERB SAUCE

Preparation time:
15 minutes

Serves 4

Calories:
21 per portion

YOU WILL NEED:
1 large garlic clove, chopped
pinch of sea salt
150 ml/¼ pint natural yogurt
black pepper
2 tablespoons chopped mixed herbs: parsley, chives, dill and tarragon

Crush the chopped garlic to a paste in a mortar. Add a pinch of salt and continue to pound. Beat in the yogurt gradually, pounding all the time. When all is amalgamated, taste for seasoning, adding more salt and black pepper as required. Stir in the chopped herbs and chill until ready to serve.

COOK'S TIP

This is an excellent sauce to serve with stuffed green peppers or tomatoes and potato or fennel salads.

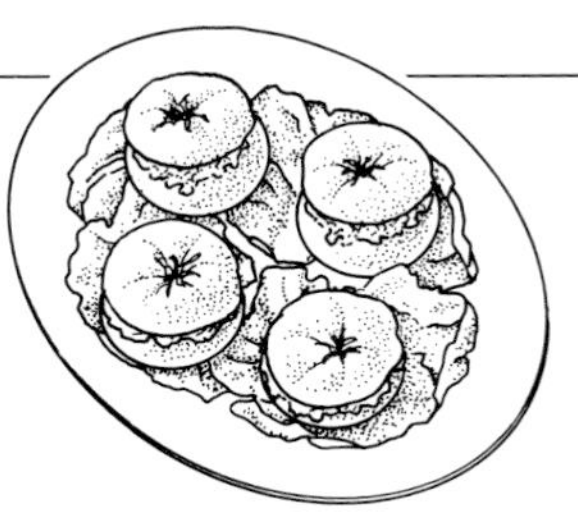

219 MAYONNAISE

Preparation time:
10 minutes

Makes:
about 150 ml/¼ pint

Total calories:
1,346

YOU WILL NEED:
1 egg yolk
¼ teaspoon each salt, pepper and dry mustard
150 ml/¼ pint olive oil
1 tablespoon white wine vinegar

Beat the egg yolk and seasoning in a bowl. Add the oil drop by drop, beating constantly. As it thickens, add the oil in a steady stream. Add the vinegar and mix thoroughly.

COOK'S TIP

For a lighter mayonnaise, replace some of the olive oil with a lighter oil like sunflower or arachide (peanut) oil.

220 LIPTAUER CHEESE DIP

Preparation time:
15 minutes

Serves 4

Calories:
80 per portion

YOU WILL NEED:
25 g/1 oz butter
175 g/6 oz low fat soft cheese
1 teaspoon Dijon mustard
1 teaspoon anchovy paste
1 teaspoon paprika pepper, plus extra for garnish
1 tablespoon chopped gherkin
1 tablespoon chopped capers
1 teaspoon finely snipped chives, plus extra for garnish
black pepper

Beat the butter until it is soft. Beat in the cheese, mustard, anchovy and paprika and beat until the mixture is smooth. Stir in the gherkin, capers and chives and season with pepper. Spoon the dip into a serving bowl and sprinkle on a little paprika and a few chopped chives to garnish.

COOK'S TIP

Crisp, colourful vegetable 'dip sticks' turn this dip into an appetising first-course salad or 'nibble' at drinks parties. Choose fresh, seasonal vegetables.

221 SESAME SEED DIP

Preparation time:
5 minutes

Serves 4

Calories:
95 per portion

YOU WILL NEED:
5 tablespoons sesame seeds
1 tablespoon sesame oil or olive oil
1 tablespoon light soy sauce
2 tablespoons dry sherry
1 teaspoon sugar
1 teaspoon malt vinegar
1 teaspoon chopped fresh coriander, to garnish

Heat the sesame seeds over a low heat in a heavy frying pan until they begin to colour.

Grind the seeds finely in a coffee grinder.

Combine the ground sesame seeds with all the remaining ingredients in a small serving bowl. If the dip seems too thick stir in a little more sherry.

Sprinkle with chopped coriander and serve with pieces of raw cucumber and mooli (Japanese radish), and blanched mangetout and French beans.

COOK'S TIP

This is an adaptation of a Chinese recipe, often used as a sauce for boiled noodles. It makes an unusual, but delicious, dip for crisp vegetables.

222 PEANUT DIP WITH CRUDITES

Preparation time:
15 minutes

Cooking time:
about 10 minutes

Serves 6

Calories:
176 per portion

YOU WILL NEED:
2 tablespoons sunflower oil
1 onion, finely chopped
2 garlic cloves, crushed
½ teaspoon chilli powder
1 teaspoon ground cumin
1 teaspoon ground coriander
6 tablespoons crunchy peanut butter
120 ml/4 fl oz water
1 teaspoon shoyu (see recipe 75)
1 teaspoon lemon juice
FOR THE CRUDITES
1 small cauliflower
1 bunch of radishes
1 red pepper, cored and seeded
6 celery sticks
6 carrots

Heat the oil in a pan, add the onion and fry until softened. Add the garlic and spices, stir and cook for 1 minute. Mix in the peanut butter, then gradually blend in the water, stirring until thickened. Add the shoyu and lemon juice and leave to cool.

Break the cauliflower into florets and halve the radishes if large. Cut the remaining vegetables into long thin pieces.

Turn the dip into a dish, place on a large plate and surround with the vegetables.

COOK'S TIP

This dip brings a hint of the Orient into salad making. Not unlike Satay sauce, it will also go well with vegetables like raw mangetout and lightly cooked green beans.

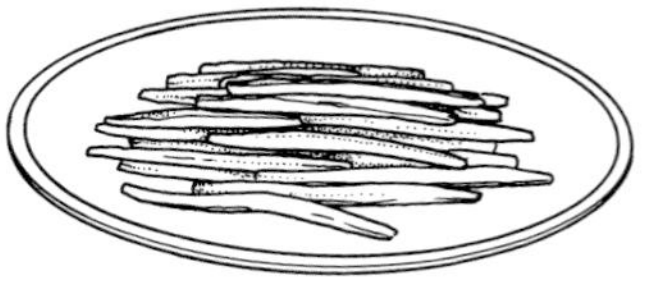

223 CELERY DIP

Preparation time:
15 minutes

Serves 4

Calories:
53 per portion

YOU WILL NEED:
175 g/6 oz low fat soft cheese
2 tablespoons natural yogurt
3 tender celery sticks, finely chopped
2 tablespoons chopped celery leaves
1 teaspoon celery seeds
salt and pepper
chopped celery leaves, to garnish

Beat the cheese and yogurt and stir in the chopped celery, leaves and seeds. Season with salt and pepper.

Spoon the dip into a serving bowl and garnish with the celery leaves.

224 BUTTER BEAN DIP

Preparation time:
15 minutes

Cooking time:
1 hour

Serves 4

Calories:
199 per portion

YOU WILL NEED:
100 g/4 oz dried butter beans, soaked overnight and drained
4 tablespoons sunflower oil
2 garlic cloves, crushed
2 tablespoons cider vinegar
2 tablespoons chopped parsley
salt and pepper
chopped parsley, to garnish

Cook the beans in boiling unsalted water for 1 hour, or until they are tender. Drain them, reserving the liquid, rinse in cold water and drain again.

Liquidize the beans in a blender with the oil, garlic, vinegar and 3 tablespoons of the reserved liquid.

Stir in the parsley and season with salt and pepper.

Garnish with the chopped parsley.

COOK'S TIP

The obvious vegetable to serve with this is celery. Also good would be slices of button mushrooms, small cauliflower florets, and raw carrot, cucumber and sweet pepper, cut in evenly matched strips.

COOK'S TIP

Both this dip and the vegetable crudités to serve with it can be prepared a day in advance and stored, each type separately, in lidded containers in the refrigerator.

225 VINAIGRETTE DRESSING

Preparation time:
10 minutes

Makes:
250 ml/8 fl oz

Total calories:
1,564

YOU WILL NEED:
175 ml/6 fl oz olive oil
2 tablespoons cider vinegar
2 tablespoons lemon juice
1 teaspoon muscovado sugar
1 garlic clove, crushed
½ teaspoon mustard
2 tablespoons chopped mixed herbs: mint, parsley, chervil, chives and thyme
salt and pepper

Put all the ingredients in a screw-top jar, adding salt and pepper to taste. Shake well to blend before serving.

COOK'S TIP

The cider vinegar here could be replaced by white wine vinegar, if preferred. Use a good quality vinegar, perhaps from Orleans.

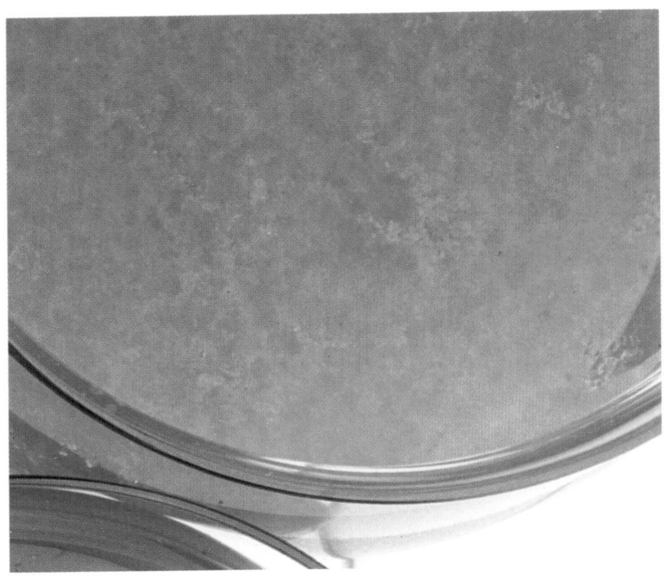

226 CURRY VINAIGRETTE

Preparation time:
5 minutes

Makes:
enough for 4 servings

Total calories:
495

YOU WILL NEED:
4 tablespoons malt vinegar
4 tablespoons sunflower oil
2 teaspoons salt
2 teaspoons curry paste

Place all the ingredients in a bowl and stir to mix thoroughly. Alternatively, shake together in a screw-top jar.

COOK'S TIP

This dressing is very good in salads which include prawns or other fish and shellfish.

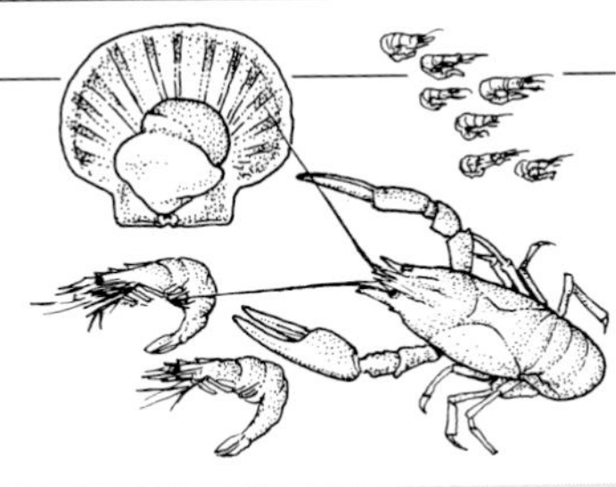

227 LEMON VINAIGRETTE

Preparation time:
5 minutes

Serves 4

Calories:
322 per portion

YOU WILL NEED:
150 ml/¼ pint olive oil
1 tablespoon wine vinegar
2 tablespoons lemon juice
grated rind of 1 lemon
1 teaspoon French mustard
salt and pepper

Place all the ingredients in a bowl and stir to mix thoroughly.

Alternatively, shake together in a screw-top jar.

228 YOGURT AND LEMON DRESSING

Preparation time:
5 minutes, plus chilling

Makes:
150 ml/¼ pint

Total calories:
80

YOU WILL NEED:
150 ml/¼ pint natural yogurt
1 tablespoon lemon juice
2 teaspoons chopped fresh herbs (see Cook's Tip)
salt and pepper

Mix the yogurt, lemon juice, appropriate herb, salt and pepper together in a bowl.

Chill for 1 hour before serving.

COOK'S TIP

To make Orange vinaigrette, use orange juice instead of lemon juice, omitting the rind.

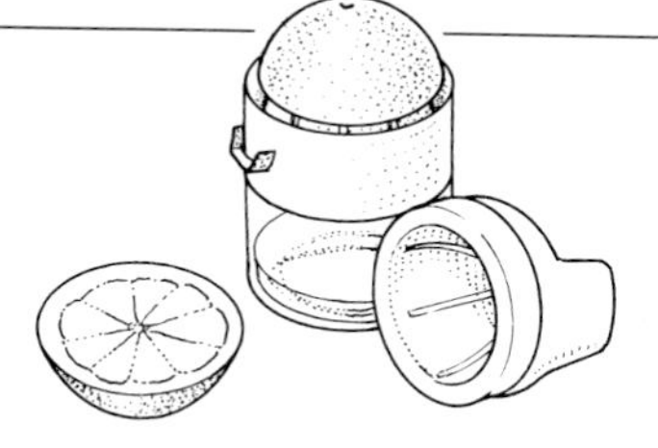

COOK'S TIP

Suggested herbs for this dressing include mint for a cucumber salad, basil for a tomato salad and a fennel for a green salad.

229 SLIMMER'S TANGY DRESSING

Preparation time:
5 minutes

Makes: 250 ml/8 fl oz

Total calories:
73

YOU WILL NEED:
250 ml/8 fl oz tomato juice
¼ teaspoon celery salt
1 teaspoon lemon juice
1 teaspoon onion, very finely chopped
¼ teaspoon Worcestershire sauce
¼ teaspoon prepared horseradish
1 garlic clove, crushed (optional)
salt and pepper
chopped shallot, to garnish

Place all the ingredients together in a small screw-top jar, cover and shake well. Use or store in the refrigerator. Shake again before using. Garnish with chopped shallot.

230 SIMPLE YOGURT DRESSING

Preparation time:
10 minutes

Makes:
300 ml/½ pint

Total calories:
153

YOU WILL NEED:
300 ml/½ pint natural yogurt
2 tablespoons lemon juice
1 garlic clove, crushed
salt and pepper

Place all the ingredients in a bowl, seasoning with ½ teaspoon salt and ½ teaspoon pepper. Mix together thoroughly. Store in an airtight container in the refrigerator until needed.

COOK'S TIP

Serve this low-calorie dressing separately, so that diners may choose for themselves how much or little to use.

COOK'S TIP

This makes a good, low-calorie alternative to mayonnaise in many salads.

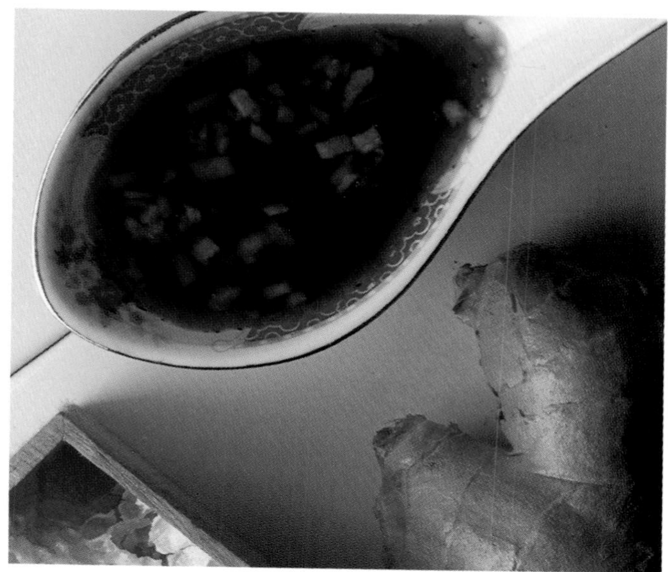

231 SOY SAUCE DRESSING

Preparation time:
5 minutes

Makes:
300 ml/½ pint

Total calories:
1,587

YOU WILL NEED:
175 ml/6 fl oz olive oil
4 tablespoons soy sauce (see Cook's Tip)
2 tablespoons lemon juice
1 garlic clove, crushed
1 cm/½ inch piece root ginger, finely chopped
salt and pepper

Put all the ingredients in a screw-top jar, adding salt and pepper to taste. Shake well to blend before serving.

COOK'S TIP

Choose the common dark variety of soy sauce for this dressing; shoyu, a naturally fermented soy sauce made from soya beans plus wheat or barley, could also be used.

232 MINT AND HONEY DRESSING

Preparation time:
5 minutes

Makes:
150 ml/¼ pint

Total calories:
482

YOU WILL NEED:
2 tablespoons clear honey
4 tablespoons cider vinegar
3 tablespoons olive oil
1 tablespoon chopped mint
salt and pepper

Put all the ingredients in a screw-top jar, adding salt and pepper to taste. Shake well to blend before serving.

COOK'S TIP

Cider vinegar has a strong, distinctive flavour and makes a refreshing vinaigrette for serving with such sharply flavoured foods as fresh tomatoes.

233 FRENCH DRESSING

Preparation time:
5 minutes

Makes:
250 ml/8 fl oz

Total calories:
1,561

YOU WILL NEED:
175 ml/6 fl oz olive oil
4 tablespoons wine vinegar
1 teaspoon Meaux mustard
1 garlic clove, crushed
1 teaspoon clear honey
salt and pepper

Put all the ingredients in a screw-top jar, adding salt and pepper to taste. Shake well before serving.

COOK'S TIP

Use either red or white wine vinegar in this dressing, choosing a good quality French vinegar.

234 SHOYU DRESSING

Preparation time:
5 minutes

Makes:
300 ml/½ pint

Total calories:
1,566

YOU WILL NEED:
175 ml/6 fl oz oil
2 tablespoons shoyu (see recipe 75)
2 tablespoons lemon juice
2 garlic cloves
pepper

Choose a light vegetable oil. Place it and the other ingredients in a screw-top jar and shake well to blend.

When using the dressing, make sure that the whole garlic cloves, used to flavour the dressing, do not go into the salad.

COOK'S TIP

For Ginger dressing, add a 2.5 cm/1 inch piece of fresh root ginger, finely chopped, to the ingredients.

235 AIOLI

Preparation time:
20-25 minutes

Serves 4

Calories:
671 per portion

YOU WILL NEED:
4 garlic cloves, chopped
2 egg yolks
pinch of salt
300 ml/½ pint olive oil
1½ tablespoons white wine vinegar

Pound the garlic in a mortar with a pestle until reduced to a pulp, or crush the garlic, then pound it with the back of a wooden spoon in a bowl. Add the egg yolks and continue to pound until thoroughly blended.

Add the salt, then start to add the oil very gradually, drop by drop, beating constantly with a wooden spoon. Once half the oil is used up, add the remainder a little more quickly, in a slow trickle, beating constantly.

When all the oil is absorbed, gradually add the vinegar, stirring constantly until well blended. Serve the Aïoli in a bowl.

COOK'S TIP

This classic Provençal garlic sauce could be made in a food processor, if preferred. All the ingredients should be used at room temperature.

236 GREEN HERB DRESSING

Preparation time:
15 minutes

Makes:
300 ml/½ pint

Total calories:
349

YOU WILL NEED:
25 g/1 oz parsley
15 g/½ oz mint
15 g/½ oz chives
3 sorrel leaves, chopped
150 ml/¼ pint natural yogurt
2 tablespoons olive oil
juice of ½ lemon
1 teaspoon clear honey
1/2 teaspoon salt
1/4 teaspoon pepper

Remove the stalks from the parsley and mint. Place the leaves in an electric blender or food processor with the remaining ingredients and blend until smooth.

Transfer the dressing to a screw-top jar. Shake it well before using.

COOK'S TIP

This amount of dressing should dress several salads. It will keep well in the refrigerator for up to one week.

237 VINAIGRETTE WITH MIXED HERBS

Preparation time:
15 minutes

Serves 4

Calories:
744 per portion

YOU WILL NEED:
salt and pepper
½ teaspoon Dijon mustard
½ teaspoon sugar
1½ tablespoons white wine vinegar
6 tablespoons olive oil
½ tablespoon lemon juice
½ teaspoon chopped tarragon
½ teaspoon chopped borage (optional)
½ teaspoon chopped lemon balm (optional)
1 teaspoon chopped chervil
1 teaspoon chopped dill
2 teaspoons chopped chives
1 garlic clove

Put a pinch of salt, preferably sea salt, in a bowl, then a few turns of the pepper mill. Add the mustard and sugar, then pour on the vinegar and stir to dissolve the seasonings. Add the oil gradually, beating well with a wooden spoon to make an emulsion.

Finally, add the lemon juice and stir in the chopped herbs. Any suitable mixture can be used. Borage and lemon balm, for instance, are optional; they are traditional herbs for flavouring salads in Germany and other central European countries. Add a peeled clove of garlic and stand for 1 hour; before using, discard the garlic.

COOK'S TIP

This vinaigrette can be mixed directly in the salad bowl. The salad ingredients can be dropped in on top of the dressing, then all tossed together.

238 TOMATO JUICE DRESSING

Preparation time:
5 minutes

Makes:
300 ml/½ pint

Total calories:
67

YOU WILL NEED:
300 ml/½ pint tomato juice
1 tablespoon tarragon vinegar
1 garlic clove, crushed
salt and pepper

In a screw-topped jar shake together the tomato juice, tarragon vinegar and garlic. Season to taste with salt and pepper. Chill before use.

COOK'S TIP

This makes a colourful, tangy, low-calorie dressing for green leaf salads. The garlic may be omitted, if preferred.

239 SLIMMER'S MAYONNAISE

Preparation time:
10 minutes

Makes:
300 ml/½ pint

Total calories:
300

YOU WILL NEED:
1 rounded tablespoon cornflour
1 teaspoon celery seed
1 teaspoon dry mustard
1 teaspoon salt
250 ml/8 fl oz semi-skimmed milk
2 egg yolks, beaten
50 ml/2 fl oz vinegar
sugar, to sweeten (optional)

Mix together the cornflour, celery seed, mustard and salt in a small heavy-based saucepan. Add the milk a little at a time and cook over a low heat, stirring constantly, until the mixture thickens. Continue to cook for 2 minutes. Cool slightly, add the beaten egg yolks and cook for a further 2-3 minutes. Remove from the heat and stir in the vinegar and sugar, if using. Chill before serving.

COOK'S TIP

This cooked mayonnaise can be stored in the refrigerator for up to two weeks.

240 YOGURT DRESSING

Preparation time:
10 minutes

Serves 4

Calories:
30 per portion

YOU WILL NEED:
150 ml/¼ pint natural yogurt
1 teaspoon caster sugar
3 teaspoons lemon juice
2 teaspoons French mustard
1 teaspoon mixed dried herbs
3 tablespoons gherkins, finely chopped
salt and pepper

In a small bowl mix together the yogurt, sugar, lemon juice, mustard and dried herbs. Add the finely chopped gherkins and season to taste. Chill before using.

COOK'S TIP

To reduce the calories in this dressing even more replace the sugar with 1 or 2 drops of liquid artificial sweetener (or omit the sweetener altogether!).

INDEX